Finding Hope Beyond the Choice

A Collective of Hope

D1260058

ISBN: 979-8-9856988-0-0

Published by:

Narratus Creative | Narratus Press
P.O. Box 1413
Hamilton, OH 45012
narratuscreative.com

Interior design: Narratus Creative
Cover Illustrated by: Ashley North

Produced in the United States of America

Dedication

For each of our children, here on earth and in heaven.

Hope deferred makes the heart sick, but a
longing fulfilled is a tree of life.
—*Proverbs 13:12 (*NIV*)*

Inside

Foreword

Abortion is generally not a topic of conversation—at least not in my world. I've heard it talked about in the News. I've listened to the debate: Pro Life vs. Pro Choice. I know about Roe v. Wade. I've seen the short films that beg to inform a distant church. I've had friends who strongly considered abortion but made the hard decision to parent. As a Christian, I have marched in the Sanctity of Life rallies because I understood it was the right thing to do. I've prayed, asking God to forgive our land for allowing abortion to continue—but I always managed to keep the gravity of abortion at a distance—until now.

I've known Machelle Montgomery for more than 26 years. Most of those years have been from several states away as my husband's work moved us just a few years after Machelle and I met. I met her while she was in the throes of healing. I understood that there was something going on inside her heart. I could visibly see her, week after week, working through issues as she fervently prayed and brought her burden to the Lord. I just didn't understand the depth of her pain. I couldn't see the layers of bondage that she was pummeling through. To be honest, once I understood she was working through the aftermath of having an abortion, I couldn't relate, so I didn't think there was much that I could do but pray.

Six months ago Machelle contacted me about working on a book she was compiling—a collaboration of stories from both women and men who have been through abortion. There really was no question about being involved. We met and the stories began trickling in. Each one different. Each one coming from a different place in life—young, old, addicted, in their right-mind, mentally unstable, affluent, underprivileged—I could go on.

Though each chapter came from a different backstory, there were many parallels that united this collection—freedom, forgiveness, redemption, grace, truth, healing, hope—again, I could go on.

Chapter after chapter, my eyes were filled with tears as I was able to be acquainted with just a bit of the grief and pain shared by each woman and man. The brutal honesty that speaks through each person's writing felt like a gut-punch, but I understood that these were stories that needed to told.

At the same time, by the end of each chapter my heart was rejoicing with more tears, only this time the tears came because each person was walking the path to a life of freedom.

I can no longer unsee how abortion affects human beings. I can no longer ignore the fact that abortion touches one in three families in the United States. I can no longer afford to keep it out of my conversations because there are more women and more men suffering through the guilt and shame of their choice.

More than likely people aren't going to run up to you or me and confess that they've had an abortion or talk about the guilt and shame they've been carrying because they made such a choice.

But there is hope. Perhaps by my beginning to bring the aftermath of abortion into my worldview I can be aware of opportunities. Opportunities to share hope. To share this book or other books. To let someone know that, though I don't understand what they are going through, I know a collective that does.

I can help these voices to be heard and their words to be read. I can continue to pray, now with understanding or at least, empathy, that those who are suffering through the aftermath of abortion will find healing. I can ask the Lord to put people in my path that I can share this book with.

I have been made aware. Instead of looking with a critical eye, instead of bashing one side or the other, or what's worse, remaining blissfully unaware, I too can now offer hope: This Collective of Hope. Hope beyond any choice.

—Denise Chaney
Publisher

Foreword

The first time I met Machelle was in September of 2013. I was just recently named Executive Director of Life Centers. It's always been my objective, whenever I started a new role, to meet all the staff personally and hear their story.

When Machelle and I met, I asked her to tell me her story. Almost an hour later, I sat there speechless; I've never had anyone be so transparent and open with me. To hear Machelle's story, the pain, the healing and the mission that was in her heart, was breathtaking.

I had heard many sermons detailing how God uses people's stories to reflect His love and compassion to a lost world. Now, in real time, I was seeing exactly what these sermons were saying: that *all* of us have a story and each of us are to use our stories to minister to others in their time of need.

Machelle has spent over two decades working on the frontlines in the battle for the hearts and lives of thousands of women who come to Life Centers looking for hope and light. The lasting imprint on the hearts and minds of these women, as a result of Machelle being in their lives, is eternal.

The Bible teaches that His flock are to be the hands and feet of Christ. Machelle has certainly lived this command with the work she has done on behalf of the unborn and those wounded by abortion. Scripture also tells us about the "treasures" we will have on the shelves in heaven. Given the work Machelle has done on behalf of our Creator, God has His carpenters busy building more shelves for Machelle.

—Tom Shevelot
Executive Director
Life Centers

A Girl I Used to Know

CHAPTER 1 • Debbie

I would like to talk with you about a girl I used to know. She grew up in a good home with loving parents. So why did she believe she was unlovable? Could it have been from the boys in the neighborhood that took advantage of her at the age of nine? Or was it the enemy of her soul whispering in her ear? Whatever it was that made her believe the lie that she was unlovable, that lie determined her path in life.

She wanted to be loved and accepted so much that she set out to be the best at everything she did and to please everyone she was around in hopes that she could be loved. Now this determination in her wasn't all bad. It helped her to achieve good grades in school and to earn a basketball scholarship to college.

College was a whole new world with new friends and experiences. One night while out with friends she met Jeff. He was so nice and really seemed to like her so she was thrilled when he asked her back to his dorm room. She hoped that he would show her the love she so desired. She gave him what he wanted in hopes of seeing him again.

She didn't see him again and four weeks later she found out she was pregnant. She didn't know what to do. As she sat in her dorm room crying, all these thoughts kept racing through her mind. *I can't let everyone know that I slept with someone I barely knew. They will think I'm a horrible person. If my parents find out they will be so disappointed in me... And how is it going to look when I lose my scholarship?* The girl couldn't let anyone know what she had done because it would prove that she really *was* unlovable.

While struggling with what to do, her roommate offered the help she thought she needed by volunteering to take her to the clinic in the next town to have an abortion. This seemed like the only option. Nobody would need to know.

As they drove to the clinic the girl kept thinking, *It will be okay. I'm not doing anything illegal so it must be okay, right?* Yet her heart was telling her this was wrong.

A Very Different Girl

The clinic was nice and the staff very friendly. The girl joined a group of about 15 women, who were there to get an abortion. The women were told they would be meeting with the counselor first so they were all escorted into a room with chairs in a circle. Each of the women was asked how she got pregnant. They were never counseled on other options or were given any type of counsel at all. Once they all shared their stories, they were told to wait their turn to be called back.

When it was her turn to go back, she was afraid and knew deep in her heart she was about to do something very wrong. She began crying as the nurse led her back to change into her gown and to get on a table in front of this big machine. When the doctor came in, he didn't speak to the girl or acknowledge her in any way. The nurse kept trying to console her, but she just kept crying. When the procedure was over, she went to the recovery room where some of the other women were resting. It was so quiet, except for her crying. This upset one of the other women, who said that if she didn't want to get the abortion, then she shouldn't have done it and she should stop her crying.

She left the clinic that day a very different girl. Nothing mattered anymore. She was numb to everything around her. She would get up and go to class and basketball practice, but she was just going through the motions. Her coach noticed the difference in her and called her to the office. She was given the option to do better or give her position to someone who would appreciate it. That day she quit the team and went back to her dorm room. The girl made the decision that she no longer wanted to live. She went through her roommate's belongings. Finding where her roommate kept all of her prescription medication, the girl took it all and lay down on her dorm room bed, hoping to die.

She didn't know it at the time but God had other plans for her. She didn't die that day, but she did get very sick and threw up everything.

After leaving college and returning home, she felt her parents disappointment, but nothing seemed to matter anymore. She still longed to be loved, but now *knew* that she didn't deserve love. She turned to drugs and alcohol and lived very recklessly. Any relationship she found herself in was abusive, but she deserved it, right? While in one of these relationships she found herself pregnant again. When she let him know he told her he didn't want to have anything to do with her or her baby. On her 21st birthday she had her second abortion. She felt dead inside.

Something to Live For

When she met Joe and he asked her to move to Indiana with him it didn't matter to her that she had only known him for two weeks. What mattered was that maybe if she moved away, she could leave everything behind and start fresh. The girl married Joe. Their marriage was abusive in every way, reinforcing the lie that she wasn't worthy of love. She deserved it all because she was unlovable.

After one year of marriage they had a daughter. The love and protection the girl felt for her daughter gave her something to live for and it started to give her courage. Six weeks pregnant with their second daughter, her husband held her down on their bed, choking her, when something rose up in her. She knew her children didn't deserve to live in a home like that and she needed to get out. A year later she found the courage to divorce him.

When she met Steve, she wasn't sure she was ready for a committed relationship but there was something different about him. He would talk about God and church. She listened, but she wasn't really sure if she believed there *was* a God.

The girl and Steve were married and about a year and a half later. With their first child on the way, she told him she wanted to find a church so the kids could know this God that he often spoke of. When their daughter was six-months-old they found a church to attend. The second Sunday they attended she knew she needed to go to the altar. The love that she so desperately searched for began to wash over her. That was the day that God began to change *that girl into me.*

That girl *was* me.

I wanted to know everything about God! I knew He was loving but when it came to my abortions and what I had done, I only felt the shame and guilt of it all. *How could God forgive me? I can't take it back and I can't fix it! How could He forgive me?* I prayed everyday for His forgiveness for my abortion but the shame and guilt stayed.

One time during my devotions, I was reading about the woman who broke the alabaster box. It had oil inside and she used to anoint the feet of Jesus. She was crying and used her tears to wash His feet. The Pharisees were judging Jesus, as well as the woman. His response to them was simple; because the woman had been forgiven of much, she loved much. This scripture helped me to know that I was forgiven, but the shame and guilt were still there. I was afraid to tell anyone what I had done. My husband was the only one who knew.

Finding Purpose in the Pain

One day I received a flyer in the mail from a crisis pregnancy center offering training classes in order to counsel women in crisis pregnancies. I had always dreamed of becoming a counselor and had been taking some Biblical counseling courses already, so I thought this would be a great opportunity. At the end of the classes one of the directors shared that if you had an abortion, there was a study group called GRACE (now called SOAR), that you would have to attend before you would be able to counsel women. I nervously approached the director to let her know that I would need to participate in the GRACE study group.

When I started the group, I went into it thinking that I was just fine. God had forgiven me and this study was just another opportunity to learn more about helping other women. What I soon found out was that I wasn't "fine". I still had a lot of things to work through. Not only was there shame and guilt, but I realized I had some anger towards the legal system because they made it so easy to go have an abortion.

At the end of the study we were told there would be a memorial service to honor our children. During the service we would have an opportunity to go up and light a candle representing our child and say something.

Sitting with my husband waiting for the service to begin, we were looking through the program. He leaned over to me and wanted to know who were all the people there. You see, there were 30 babies being honored that day. The gravity of that moment is one I will not forget. My "pregnancies" became people in that moment. People who had a purpose and a plan for their life. A plan I chose to take away from them.

I was so nervous and a little afraid to go up and light those candles. So much so that all I could manage to get out were their names. I wanted to say so much more, like how sorry I was and how I loved them. Yet walking back to my seat I felt God delivering me from the shame and guilt. It is hard to describe, but it was like this huge weight was just lifted off. I was free!!!

This, I believe, is the freedom that God has called us to in order that we may serve others. Galatians 5:13 (ESV) says, "For you were called to freedom brothers. Only do not use your freedom as an opportunity for the flesh, but through love serve one another."

It is for this very reason that it is my privilege to now help facilitate the SOAR (formally called GRACE) groups.

That girl who thought she was unlovable? That girl was me, but she no longer has a voice. By God's grace and mercy she has become a new creation. I know that I am loved, forgiven and free!

Debbie Decker is currently a Licensed Minister through the Assembly of God and Womens Ministry leader in her local church. Discipling new believers and facilitating the abortion recovery groups called Soar are a few of her passions. She has been blessed with three beautiful daughters and seven grandchildren.

My Most Tragic Decision

CHAPTER 2 • Fran

*T*o tell of the most tragic decision of my life is not easy; for I betrayed myself and everything I believe in.

If I would try to sum up in one word what led to my abortion it would be: insecurity. Growing up I felt as though I was always on the outside looking in, wanting so desperately to belong but never fitting in. Try as hard as I could, I would just never measure up.

Family Matters

I was raised in a neighborhood with 33 homes and we were one of the only two Catholic families. Of the rest, only six other homes went to church and only four of them had children. In short there was not a big godly influence from the people with whom we associated. When I was around the age of five I was molested, but to this day I have not recalled who it was. This skewed my view on the world around me and the view I had of myself and sex. I don't know if it was instinctive, but I knew what had happened was bad and I felt dirty. I was different.

I was expected to go to Mass on Sunday (which I generally did by myself) and five days a week at school before classes began. Therefore my religious instruction came from the nuns and church, not at home. At my house a strong work ethic, respect for authority and being reliable was stressed. My mother would tell me that I was the responsible one because I kept my room clean, did my homework without being told, and helped her around the house. I was raised on these adages: "You can't expect something for nothing"; "No one owes you anything"; and "If you want to eat, you have to work." My parents were from the Great Depression and did not believe in owing anyone anything. My siblings and I had shelter, food and clothing, but there was never a lot of emotional support. The only family events were reunions and one time we went to a drive-in movie. I never went to my parents with my hurts, fears or concerns. It never came across my mind. Instead I tried to navigate the world on my own.

Like many families, our home was dysfunctional. My mother stayed home and worked with the meager budget my father gave her, and although my dad worked, he was gone in the evenings. He avoided the conflict at home by being on a bowling team or going to my grandmother's or one of his relatives. My mother would take her frustration out on us kids. My eldest brother was thirteen years older than me and my sister was nine years older than me so by the time I was nine, they were out of the house. My mother hated my father and his mother. One of her derisive remarks to me would be to tell me that I was just like them—my father's family.

I hung my head for most of my life because of this, apologetic for who I was. However when I would go to family reunions I couldn't understand why the rest of my relatives didn't feel ashamed. If we were so terrible, how could they laugh and enjoy themselves. Many years later when I was in my 50s, my mother made that comment to me one more time. At that moment it occurred to me that she was right. I *am* 50% my father's family and I told her so. "I am 50% my father's family. I have their DNA so I probably do act like them." I reminded her that she had made that decision (choosing my father), I did not. I was done apologizing.

I have said all this to explain that I was very insecure from an early age. When my parents separated I was nine years old. I had never heard of "divorce" and no one bothered to explain what it was or how it would affect our family. I came home to find my father moving out; no one else was there. While he was packing I brought him my school picture and asked him not to forget me. I thought he wouldn't be my dad anymore. I did continue to see him on visitations every other weekend.

After the divorce I was on my own. My mother worked and there was no one else at home, so I babysat to earn money. I started hanging around with older kids and married couples. I was smoking and drinking alcohol, but by the grace of God drugs did not come into the picture.

Confused Love

When I was 14 I met my first love. He was 4 years older than me.

He showed me attention and affection which lead to sex, and although I knew it was wrong, I justified it because he loved me. So at age 16 I was pregnant and married (no it was not a shot gun service, he was free to leave). Once married, he had several jobs and multiple affairs, which only fueled my insecurity. Just before my 17th birthday, I gave birth to a beautiful baby girl. I thought that now that we had a baby my husband would change and become responsible. Of course, I was naive. Finally, after discovering more affairs, I'd had enough and filed for divorce, which I received for my 18th birthday.

Being young, I confused love with sex, not realizing that sex cannot bring love. At 20, I met someone at work who was more grounded and responsible, someone like me who was a hard worker. I felt we had more in common. When I got pregnant, he wanted no part of having a baby and said he would pay for the abortion. Here I was again, pregnant before marriage, covered in guilt and shame, feeling trapped with no way out. I was already caring for one child and living with my mother without any financial support from my ex-husband. How could I take care of two children? How could I possibly tell my father? I had already shamed him once. I felt abortion was my only solution.

I knew when I walked into the clinic that I didn't want to be there. I met a young girl in the waiting room and we began talking. She told me it was not a big deal; this was her third. All I could feel was sadness because I knew that living inside me was a baby. I have often wondered about that young girl and if she was able to have any children later in her life. When I went back to the sterile, white room, a nurse spoke calmly and smiled saying it would all be over quickly. I was in my first trimester. When they suctioned my baby out of the safety of the womb that should have sheltered and protected him or her, there was physical, emotional and spiritual pain. I knew I had let my little one pay the price for my guilt and shame.

My mother and sister knew about the abortion, but no one else. It was never spoken of again. I went back to work and moved on with life as if nothing had happened; but it had happened and I would never be the same. To this day most of my family does not know about my abortion. I remember at 21-years-old telling my mother that I was going to hell and there was nothing I could do about it. I completely and totally believed it. I murdered my baby; of course I was going to hell. O, but God!

The young man and I dated about 2 more years, but we broke up when I got saved.

A Solid Foundation

I got saved in 1977 and it took many years, brick by brick to tear down the walls that I had built to protect myself. In 1983, I married the love of my life and we have been married 38 years. Bill accepted me, loved me, cherished me and allowed God to use him in helping to heal my insecurities. We each had a child when we married, ages eleven and four, so we agreed not to have a child together. I was relieved. I didn't want to have a child because I had broken trust with the Sacred and myself. I would have felt like I was having a replacement baby and nothing could ever replace the child I aborted.

I always worried that if someone at church discovered my past that they would no longer want to associate with me or let me take care of their babies in the nursery. In 1986, I began going to Southwest Church of God where I met Machelle Montgomery. A few years later she shared her abortion experience with the congregation and how God healed her. She began a class on post abortion. I went, but I did not receive the freedom that God had given her.

When my daughter was in college she was doing a paper on abortion. I walked in her room and there were pictures of aborted babies. I felt like the oxygen had been sucked out of the room. I asked her if she thought a woman who had an abortion could be saved and her reply was, "Mom that is the only way she could live with herself." I later told my daughter about the abortion.

Several years passed and I began attending Plainfield First Assembly of God. There I met Debbie Decker, who is currently a facilitator with SOAR (at that time it was called GRACE). Debbie spoke one Sunday about an upcoming GRACE class so I went to see her. At the same time one of our young ladies, Esther, asked if I would be her spiritual mentor. Esther was 18, so I said, "First I need to tell you I have had an abortion and you may want to change your mind." She sweetly looked up at me and said, "Jesus forgave you so it is under the blood." To be sure there would be no offense and that I wouldn't be over-stepping, I checked with her mother, Cindy. She virtually said the same thing. Their compassion and kindness gave me the strength I needed to go forward with GRACE. This is when I shared with Bill I had an abortion.

In one of my GRACE sessions, the Holy Spirit showed me how the shame I was carrying was a burden that Jesus had already paid for on the Cross. This was an epiphany to me. When I got saved I knew He forgave of my sins. I didn't doubt it. I knew he took my guilt, but somehow I felt the shame was mine to bear. When I realized Jesus took my shame as well, I started crying and praising God in the Spirit. It took 60 years to get there, but I was finally free.

I will always live with the regret of my decision. My precious unborn child did not get to have their chance at life. Who knows who they would have become or how they would have contributed to life on earth? I don't know my child's name, but God does and I am thankful that I will get to meet her or him when I get home.

I am sharing this—my story—hoping that if someone is considering abortion they won't go through with it, or if they have had one, they will turn to Jesus for salvation and receive the deliverance they so desperately need.

Fran Burrows is retired after 40 years in the workforce and is living with her husband Bill in Mooresville, Indiana. They have two grown daughters and two beautiful grandchildren.

The Wages of Sin is Death

CHAPTER 3 • TaShaya

I believe in Christ. I know that the wages of sin *is* death. I never imagined that I would kill my first unborn child. I did not know my sinful lifestyle would bring me to aborting a gift God gave me. My sins produced death, an abortion. I went to church and Sunday school. I was baptized. I believe in the Trinity. Yet, my selfishness ruled me. My self-centered mentality dictated my decision to take a life.

It would be seven years later, as a married woman, before I experienced the joy of having a child, my third pregnancy. You see, in my second pregnancy my body opened at 20 weeks and there was nothing more the doctors could do. A cerclage (a single stitch around the cervix to prevent miscarriage) was not an option. I was already six-to-seven centimeters dilated.

I knew that day, that either this little life I had known for five months would enter the earth healthy or return to God. Whichever way, I was okay because I had another opportunity to carry life within my body. I shared space with this little person and was so grateful that God had given me another chance. At first, it was a chance I did not feel I deserved.

Because God is my friend, He told me before He took my baby's spirit that my baby was returning with Him. I was okay and I knew that my baby no longer resided within my physical body. He returned to God. It was not until the next morning, when I reflected on David and Bathsheba's story, that my husband and I found peace in saying goodbye to this life we knew for five short months. Baby Trey: *Mommy and Daddy love you very much. One day we will see you again in eternity and be together.*

Remembering Zion, My First

I recall getting off the telephone with the baby's father wondering, *How am I going to cut him out of my life?* At that very moment, I knew I was with child. I took several pregnancy tests and hoped and even prayed that I was not pregnant, but I was. Roughly five weeks pregnant. I called and set an appointment with the clinic to abort my first pregnancy. I was told the amount and we set the date. I was seven weeks pregnant when I made the decision to end Zion's life. As I sat in that room and looked around, I recall praying for the few women there with me. I knew in my spirit I would recover, but I was so terrified for them. I had no clue the emotional devastation that awaited me as a result of this decision: my lack of forgiving myself, the guilt and the depression that stayed too long in my life.

When I left that clinic, I was mostly silent on the ride home, as I had no words. It took weeks for my body to recover. I could barely walk. I was in physical pain. My body changed. My mind was not at rest. I felt like a dark cloud was over my head pouring rain on me. My thoughts became weapons. I was destroying myself. I was tormented mentally, emotionally and spiritually.

After recovering and returning to work, I sat at my desk and wept as I had never wept before. The tears would not stop. I was so afraid that a coworker would ask me, "Why the tears?" I knew I could not lie. I knew I would be compelled to tell someone. I had taken a life and I was not okay. I Googled "help after an abortion" and found GRACE. I quickly called and set an appointment.

Emergency Surgery

When I entered Machelle's office, all I could do was cry. I think I used a whole box of tissues within that hour. I felt like a levee had broken. I could not contain my tears. I went through the healing classes that were offered. Each week God's Word began to do emergency surgery on me. When I looked back at the end of the course, I thought, *Wow! God just healed me through His Word every week*. It was kind of sneaky, yet I was incredibly grateful. He truly turned my mourning into dancing. I was free. It was not a secret. I did not go broadcasting *how* he set me free, but I was not bound like months prior.

Almost two years later my pastor would ask me to speak on a Sunday morning about singleness. I had no idea that when I spoke I would reveal that the wages of sin *is* death. I told the church in two services that my sins caused me to take a baby's life. I wagered a life because I sinned. God blessed me with a platform to gain more freedom and to help others. My abortion was not a secret that the devil could use to blackmail me anymore.

After the services, I was surprised at the women and men who came for prayer and to talk to me. My brief testimony, or snippet, of my experience helped so many that day.

God, I am grateful that You are using me to help others Thank You for healing me to help others.

Five years later, in the middle of a pandemic, God allowed Caleb Maximus to enter this world. He is our rainbow baby for sure. The joy we have, the world did not give it to us, GOD did.

Father in Heaven, we thank You for Your mercy and kindness towards us.

God forgives. Forgive yourself too.

TaShaya Mayfield is a native of Gary, IN and attended high school in Indianapolis, IN. She graduated from Indiana State University with her undergraduate degree in Journalism and achieved her master's degree from Indiana Wesleyan in Management and Human Resources. She is an Adjunct Professor for a community college and a Federal Agent for the U.S. Government. She has spent the last 10 years building two careers in helping others. She works with

individuals to encourage and motivate them to the greatness they have dreamed of having. She is married to her high school sweetheart and God blessed them to raise three children and their nephew together. She enjoys traveling the world and meeting new people along the way. Her favorite scripture is Psalm 91. A prayer of protection that she believes in.

Good Girl

CHAPTER 4 • *Ashley*

rowing up, I made sure to manage my external reputation by maintaining my definition of a "good girl" image. Sure, I made some bad mistakes, but in my mind, if I didn't drink, use drugs or have sex before marriage, God and others would love me, be proud of me and want to be in relationship with me. Being an athlete from the age of five, performing to earn approval and love came naturally to me. Performing well became integral to every part of my life. High school came and went and I found myself at college with no idea who I was as a person or what I was meant to do, other than play basketball.

My parents divorced when I was 19, and my relationship with my Dad started to become strained. At the same time the grandmother that I was closest to had been diagnosed with cancer and within five months. We had been in and out of church over the years, but I hadn't formed a strong faith of my own. My family had been my constant foundation and this foundation quickly crumbled beneath my feet in devastating and traumatic fashion. In the chaos and grief that ensued, I chose to run away from God rather than run toward Him.

By my junior year in college I craved attention, affirmation and value from men more and more. At 21, I gave myself away for the first time to someone I considered a close friend. From there, I lived a lifestyle of sexual brokenness, going from one partner to another. The intense shame I experienced kept growing and the gap between where I was and where I wanted to be was ever widening. The "good girl" image was still portrayed outwardly, but inwardly, I felt lost, dirty, used, misunderstood and abandoned.

My senior year of college was ending and I had no plans for the future. I wasn't going to graduate on time because I had all but thrown away a year and a half of my education on distractions. I didn't want to be an elementary school teacher anymore, but I didn't know what career to commit to and pursue. I was still running from God, or at least, the image of God created through my distorted lens. I believed

He had given up on me. *What kind of God would want to love someone like me?* I knew how selfish and out of control my life was. I hated who I had become and figured that if anyone knew what I really was like, in all of my darkness, they'd hate me too —God included.

The summer of my 22nd year brought with it two pink lines on a pregnancy test. Shock and disbelief flooded my heart and mind. *How could I have been so foolish and careless?* Almost right away, I knew the decision I would make. I was in a prison of shame and fear that I helped to build with my poor decisions. I didn't see a way out of my temporary circumstances other than abortion. I could only hear fear on every side.

Unsure of how to get an abortion, I made one phone call to a friend and confessed my messed-up life. I was met with kindness, understanding and the sentiment that I would be supported if abortion is what I chose to do. I received that same response from my boyfriend at the time. *What did I even know about abortion?* I was the girl who never expected to have sex before marriage, let alone get pregnant. There was no time to be transparent or tell anyone else. I knew that if either one of my parents knew, they would do everything in their power to not let me get an abortion. So, without talking to anyone else, my aforementioned friend made the phone call to set up an abortion appointment.

Befriending Shame

There was a big waiting room and then a smaller one at Planned Parenthood. When I was taken back for an ultrasound, I didn't look at the screen because I wasn't more than eight or nine weeks along. After all, I wouldn't be able to see anything because it was just a clump of cells, right? I went into the smaller room with about a half-dozen other women waiting for their abortions. Several of them were talking to each other and sharing the reasons for their decision. I stayed silent, still not sure of how I got there or what was to come in the procedure room.

I don't remember much about the procedure room, other than the cold, hard table and that there was a clock on the wall. I didn't look at the instruments that were to be used. I laid down. The doctor came in, made some sort of joke to try and lighten the mood, chuckled at his attempt to make me laugh and then got to work. I pushed away any maternal or humane instincts that tried to pierce my conscience. As I held the nurse's hand, silent tears flowed down my cheeks while my first child was gruesomely ripped from my body.

No one talked in the recovery room. We all sat there, each woman silently processing the trauma they just endured. My relief lasted maybe two seconds and then horror flooded my heart. *If this was just a clump of cells in my body, why did I feel like a monster?*

After my first abortion, I became even more inwardly shame-filled and angry. I was afraid that if I let myself feel anything after my abortion, I would never be able to live under the weight of it all. The shame and disgust were unbearable to think about, so I decided to become numb inside. And then, I went right back into the sexual brokenness that had led me to the worst decision of my life.

In the ten months that followed, I got pregnant two more times and each time, made the decision to abort. My second abortion was called a medical abortion, which meant that I took the abortion pills, my baby died in my womb, and then came out at home. I bled horribly for days, and eventually had to go to the hospital because I was afraid something was wrong. The doctor I saw gave a disapproving look when I told her the reason for my visit, but said I would be fine. Though I would recover physically, something was still very wrong. I was ending the lives of my babies, continuing in my promiscuous lifestyle, almost daring God to let me get pregnant again. So, pregnant for a third time, I found myself at the abortion clinic, saying goodbye to yet another baby in the most violent way.

My womb was supposed to be the safest place on earth for my babies, but I had made it a place of death. I had literally and figuratively killed off any desire for motherhood. I continued to befriend guilt, shame, regret, fear and despair because there seemed like no other option.

The Huddle

A couple of years had passed when a former teammate reached out to me about a potential job coaching basketball at a Christian school. I got the job.

I put my hand in the huddle at the end of my first basketball practice as an assistant coach and immediately felt exposed. Over a dozen pairs of eyes were looking at me, having no idea that this single interaction was quietly upsetting my internal world. I accepted the job hoping to enjoy the game I loved once again; instead, God would use it to change my life.

By this time, I had been attending a church, though I was sure God wanted nothing to do with me. Still, it seemed like the right thing to do. God was trying to get my attention. I somehow knew in that God ordained huddle-moment, He was telling me it was time to stop running and trying to hide. He saw me. Now I had young girls seeing me as a leader in their lives.

Here I was, coaching at a Christian school and claiming to be a follower of Jesus at one time in my life, yet how was I supposed to be a good example when I was a complete mess? Not long after I started coaching, I began dating a man who was a Christian believer. Although I was convinced he would break up with me immediately, I felt it best to confide in him about my sexual brokenness and my abortions. My confession was received with grace and tenderness. He suggested I share my story with his mom, as he believed that God did not abandon me because of my sin.

I was invited to dinner at his mom's home. Kelly received me and had compassion on me as she would her own daughter. Her dinner table is the first place where I found out that God loved me, wholly and completely, and wanted to bring healing and life where there had only been darkness and death. She suggested I try and find a support group for women who have had abortions, so that is what I did. I Googled "after abortion help" and the GRACE (now called SOAR) Bible study through Life Centers was the first thing I saw.

A New Trajectory

I drove past the meeting place for my initial conversation with Machelle, the director of the study. I sat in a parking lot for a few minutes and thought that maybe I could just keep running from God and not face what I had done. Thankfully, God gave me the courage to take a deep breath and keep the meeting. Machelle shared her story with me; I told her why I was there; and we made plan for my participation in the Bible study. There would be five meetings and then a weekend retreat.

A small circle of chairs greeted me in my first Bible study meeting. I felt sick to my stomach because being that close to people while talking about my abortions was the very last thing I wanted to do! It was an emotional yet powerful few weeks, as we became vulnerable with our facilitators and each other. The study was a safe place for us to let our walls down long enough to be honest. We were open about where our stories had taken us away from God, then we allowed Him to show us the enormity of His forgiveness for us and His desire for His daughters to come home into His arms.

During one of the prayer times at the weekend retreat, all of the emotions that I had tried to numb and never feel again came pouring out in sobs as I knelt on the floor. It was then that Jesus reminded me of what He did for me on the Cross. Either He died for all of my sins, including me taking the lives of my babies, or He died for none of them. I was flooded with gratitude for this forgiveness. A forgiveness that I would never be able to pay back. I was undone by the love He was showing to me. I had done the unthinkable, yet there He was, looking at me with a grace and a compassion in His eyes that changed the trajectory of my life. No one had ever loved me like Jesus. I truly became born-again.

Memorial Sunday was the last part of the retreat weekend. We were asked to name and honor our children. To memorialize them in a way to show that they existed; that they are loved; and that they are embraced eternally by our Father in heaven. I had a quiet, reassuring understanding in my heart: *two girls, one boy*. I wasn't sure how far along I was with any of my babies at the time of my abortions, so I needed God to give me insight as to their gender, and He did. I named my children Abigail, James and Isabella (little Bella).

No More Performance

I was set free from shame that weekend, and part of the overflow of that deliverance was the ability to go up to the front of the room to light three candles in memory of my children. I spoke their names out loud for the first time in front of a room full of people who could understand not only my pain, but also understand my newfound joy in receiving the love of Jesus.

The study, *Forgiven and Set Free,* from the GRACE study began to replace the lies I had believed with the everlasting truths found in the Word of God. Healing, freedom and restoration isn't a one-time occurrence though. This is a continual journey of saying, "Yes" to Jesus. For me, it started with being open and continues by being sharing the incredibly painful parts of my story with people I trust —and by saying, "Yes" to the ongoing healing process with Jesus.

I learned that I didn't have to perform in order to receive God's love, but He loved me first and my life can be a response to that love. I was able to volunteer and then work for Life Centers. This also helped my healing process tremendously because I was able to listen to and talk with women about the longer-term effects of abortion on women and men, and the reality of abortion taking the life of a child. Though I enjoyed being a listening ear, God had to remind me that there was nothing I could do to atone for my abortions. Whether a woman chose abortion or life for her child, did not determine God's level of forgiveness. His forgiveness and love was complete and based on His sacrifice for me, *not* my performance or my ability to persuade anyone to choose life.

One day at the center, I was asked to come see a nine-week-old baby on the ultrasound screen. I saw little hands and feet wiggling and heard a beautifully strong heartbeat. I went home and cried for hours. *How could I have believed only three or four years earlier that my womb contained only a clump of cells?* I had most likely flushed my second baby down the toilet while aborting at home. It was too much for me to bear, but Jesus bore it all on the cross. He didn't stop there, He came back to life after His death so that I could have new life as well.

In this new life, I am forgiven and set free, but I am also reminded that these were lives that I had lost, so grieving was and still is perfectly acceptable and appropriate. Sometimes the grief would come like waves, but God was there in each one, telling me of His great love for me and comforting me in my loss. I grieved my aborted children for 10 years, but God was doing a deep work in my heart and mind the whole time. He told me that yes, I would still grieve, but I could no longer hold onto that grief in a way that was becoming unhealthy. I wrote a letter to my children, put it in a case and threw it in a body of water to signify letting go in a way that I hadn't before.

The Reawakening

God reawakened my desire for a family and urged me to truly believe in His ability to restore and redeem my life. For years, I had written prayers and thoughts in a journal for my future husband, not knowing if a husband for me even existed. At the age of 32, I met my husband, Jason, at church. We knew early on that this was it for us, so we had our first date, got engaged and married within five months. One way that I knew for certain Jason was the man for me is that He spoke to me and looked at me like Jesus had all those years. Had I not known how God saw me and loved me, I may not have recognized Jason for who he is. After our first couple of dates, life with him just made sense. *Oh, there you are*, I thought. I had been waiting for Jason all along.

Months after we were married, my family fractured in a different, still devastating way. God had been so perfect in His timing of Jason coming into my life and I'm forever grateful for it. Though life around us was swirling with chaos and confusion, Jason and I drew closer to one another and to God. He was our solid foundation and He proved faithful through it all, even the miscarriage with our first child together.

We named our child Hope because God had spoken very clear to my heart during that time that I was still to trust in Him for life to come from my womb. Jason and I grieved together, and I was tempted to believe that our child's death was payback for my abortions. Thankfully, God's Word once again soothed my aching heart, as well as the comforting prayers and words from friends and family.

All of the tears and sorrow eventually led to a beautiful new life. Our daughter, Ana, was born in the summer of 2019, three months after the death of my dad. I realize more and more that joy and sorrow often walk together through the seasons of life. God brought indescribable joy and celebration in the birth of our daughter, even though I was in the midst of deep grief with the passing of my dad. We were blessed with another beautiful miracle in 2021 with the birth of our son, Nathan.

I never could have imagined or dreamt that God would redeem and restore so fully, but here I sit, given grace and mercy I didn't deserve or earn. There is no limit to what God can do with a yielded life. God's restoration looks differently through each of our lives, but our "Yes" to Him (which is also a gift from Him), means that truly nothing is impossible with Him. My life is but one of millions of examples of God's everlasting love and delight in His children. He can and will mend broken hearts and bring life from death. May the extravagant, abundant goodness of God be yours today in Christ Jesus.

Ashley was born, raised and currently resides in Indiana. After attending the SOAR group study, she volunteered and later worked full-time for Life Centers, a pro-life pregnancy resource center in Indianapolis. Her vocational ministry background also includes working for Anchorsaway and Outreach, Inc. Ashley is married to Jason and loves being a stay-at-home Mom with her two precious children, Ana and Nathan.

I Will Give You a New Heart

CHAPTER 5 • Angie

When I was seven years old I gave my heart to the Lord and became a Christian.

At 34-years-old, I had an abortion.

I was a single mother with two children when I was faced with an unplanned pregnancy. Instead of taking responsibility for my sin, asking God to forgive me and choosing life for my baby, I made the devastating, life-altering decision to cover my sin with another sin: destroying God's beautiful creation.

The Irony

Married in 1984, I had two beautiful babies. During my 12-year marriage I was faithful to God. I taught my babies about Jesus and we attended church every Sunday. My husband and I were having marital problems, so I prayed daily for God to preserve my family and preserve my marriage.

When my marriage ended in 1996, I was a raw nerve. I wasn't necessarily mad at God because my marriage ended, but I was finished being the "good girl". Where had it gotten me? My marriage had ended and I was a single mom. I made a conscience decision to do it my way for a change—I basically walked away from God. This was the beginning of the worst time of my life.

Looking back, if I had fallen into the loving arms of Christ instead of doing it my reckless way, being rebellious and disobedient, my story would be different today.

On Mother's Day in1998, I looked at the positive pregnancy test and started screaming. The montage of thoughts running through my mind were plentiful. *My parents cannot find out. People will think I'm a slut. This will damage my children. I'll be one of those women who has kids from different men.* I was scared. I was embarrassed. I was prideful. In my mind I thought I had to take control of the situation and fix it, and I was going to fix it, *my way*. Proverbs 16:18 (KJV) reads: "Pride goeth before destruction and a haughty spirit before a fall." I was the epitome of this verse.

With all these thoughts racing through my head at the same time, I immediately thought that in order to fix this situation, I needed an abortion. I was brazened. I was hard-hearted, cold and unloving. I already had two babies that I loved; there was no room for another. I never prayed about this decision. If I prayed and was obedient to the Holy Spirit, it would mean keeping the baby. However, this wasn't what I wanted so I never allowed myself to think about God, let alone talk to Him. I couldn't take the chance of changing my mind. I was still going to do it my way. I continued being rebellious, disobedient and prideful.

In addition, I purposely never consulted anyone who I thought might try to change my mind. I was calloused. I was going through with this. I just had to wait until I was five weeks pregnant. I'm not sure if it's this way now, but back then abortion clinics wouldn't perform abortions until the baby's heartbeat could be seen beating on an ultrasound, which is about five weeks.

Isn't it ironic that to destroy a life, that same precious life must prove its existence?

One memory that stands out to me occurred right after the abortion. The clinic provided a "recovery" room for all post-abortive women. It was a large room with about a dozen brown, faux leather, reclining chairs filled with women who were eating cookies and drinking juice. The message being conveyed by Planned Parenthood seemed to be: "All it takes to recover from killing our unborn babies is cookies, juice and a 10-minute rest in a recliner." As I sat there participating in this nauseating ruse, I thought to myself, *This is nothing more than a factory of death.*

When I left the clinic that day, my pridefulness evaporated. Initially there was a feeling of relief, but the relief was replaced with unimaginable shame, then denial. It was better to not think about it and I certainly didn't talk about it. I ran further away from God and hid my face from Him. This insidious sin I committed became my deepest darkest secret. My mind became a playground for the enemy.

The Playground

As I moved on with my life I looked the same and I acted the same, but I was forever changed. I was a shell of my former self. As the years passed, life was busy raising my children, but the abortion was always in the back of my mind. Since I lived in a constant state of shame and denial, as fast as the memory surfaced, I would force it back down and bury it deeper. I remember while driving I would often see bumper stickers such as, "Abortion stops a beating heart." When I would see one, I would do everything in my power to maneuver away from that vehicle. What I didn't realize at the time is that I was exhibiting post-abortive behavioral changes.

At some point I returned to church and remarried while continuing to raise my children. About 10 years after my abortion, I began having flashbacks from that day. I couldn't sleep. I was suffering from depression and I could no longer bury the memories when they surfaced. The Lord was nudging me and I knew that it was time to address my past.

Through Christian counseling I found some solace from my pain. I felt a sense of relief from the huge albatross hanging around my neck; it wasn't quite as heavy, but it was still hanging there. This albatross was still a deep dark secret I had to keep from my parents and loved ones. I certainly wasn't free from it.

I continued to be tormented, trying to get through the maze of my spiritual dilemma. I was afraid that if I was given the chance to go back in time, I would repeat my mistake.

How do you ask God to forgive you for a sin when He knows in my heart there's a possibility, I'd repeat the sin? Did I have true regret? There was shame, but did I truly regret having the abortion? Was I still trying to control the situation? Those thought really scared me.

I also felt shame because I knew when I decided to have the abortion that God would forgive me. Which meant that I stomped all over the precious blood of Jesus and exploited His mercy, grace and forgiveness. I was desperate to find relief from this confusion. My shame was immeasurable! I didn't know how to process this and make it right with the Lord. My mind continued to be the enemy's playground. He kept me confused, believing that I would still be that horrible person who would have the abortion again if I could go back in time. I truly believed there was no hope. Depression came fast and furious.

Seventeen years after the abortion, continuing to suffer from relentless depression, the Lord placed an answer right in my path. It was an answer to a prayer I had yet to even begin to pray. I found a beautiful Bible study specifically for post-abortive women. The sin of abortion not only destroys God's creation, it also destroys the mother. As women, God has hard-wired us to love, protect, nurture and care for our babies. When we do the exact antithesis of this (abortion) we are shattered spiritually.

Attending this Bible study, I realized that I suffered from post-abortive stress. I experienced depression, guilt, shame, flashbacks, fear of losing my living children and unworthiness, to name a few. I experienced behavioral changes as well, such as being over-protective of my living children. For example, for years I was petrified my daughter would be kidnapped, raped and murdered, and that my son would be killed in a car accident. I lived in absolute paralyzing fear at times thinking about the safety of my children, never realizing that this behavior was a direct result of my abortion and the unconscious fear of God taking them away from me.

During the SOAR Bible study, I realized that the fear I had of repeating the abortion (if I could go back in time) had nothing to do with my perceived lack of regret or remorse, but more to do with my attempt to continue to control the situation myself. I thought I had to have all my thoughts in-line. I reasoned that I had to have correct thinking before I could ever go before God with this gut-wrenching obstacle. The enemy had been wreaking havoc in my mind.

Releasing Control

Another area of this beautiful Bible study is naming your baby and providing a memorial service. These little ones are important and are worthy of our recognition. Naming my sweet baby and participating in a memorial service for him was a very spiritually profound, life-saving moment for me. Before this, I was in denial over him being my baby. It was an abortion and if it stayed an abortion without a name, I wasn't connected to him.

Once I gave a name to the baby, he became mine. He became real to me. The tears flowed. My body physically hurt and my heart was shattered and pulverized. He was real. He went from being an abortion to being my child, my flesh and blood. He was my sweet baby, Aaron William Coates! He belongs to me. He has siblings, grandparents, nieces and nephews; he is important and highly valued! He holds a place in our hearts and home.

God performed a miracle in me during this Bible study. He unlocked my confused mind, which had become a spiritual prison where the enemy was the warden. I stopped running and stood still. I turned around and there stood Jesus. Psalm 91:1 (KJV) is the perfect Bible scripture that demonstrates what happened when I stopped running and turned toward Jesus. "He who dwells in the shelter of the Most High will rest in the shadow of the Almighty." I ran into the shelter of the Most High!

God applied his Holy salve to my wounds and began to heal my heart. Ezekiel 36:26 (KJV): "I will give you a new heart and put a new spirit in you; I will remove from you your heart of stone and give you a heart of flesh."

It goes without saying, if I could go back in time, I would choose life for my baby boy. I wish I would have "dwelt in the shelter of the Most High" and prayed for God's forgiveness and direction back then. I wish I would have trusted God instead of choosing to control the situation, thinking that I knew what was best. It's impossible to go back in time, but along with a new heart, God brought me spiritual peace and the ability to walk in the freedom of His forgiveness all the while learning to "rest in the shadow of the Almighty."

No More Secrets

The Lord was moving mightily in my life once I turned to Him and sincerely asked for His forgiveness. I was listening to Him and being obedient. I felt as though I was on a fast-moving train and Jesus was the conductor. I had given up control. I was following Jesus and I knew that He was calling me to be part of the SOAR (Spiritually Oriented Abortion Recovery) Bible study ministry.

He was also telling me it was time. Time to bring my secret into the light with my parents. As I mentioned earlier, my parents were never to know about my abortion. This secret was going to my grave. The enemy loves it when we hold fast to our secrets because it allows him to torment us, holding our secrets over our head, keeping us living in fear that the secret will come out. All of this prevents us from living in the fullness of God's will.

I knew it was time to tell Mom and Dad. I had shared my story with my pastor at the time, telling him I was going to tell my parents. I mentioned how long I had kept this secret from them, but I knew the Lord wanted me to bring it out into the light. He assured me that he and his wife would be praying at the day and time I planned to talk to my parents.

During the ride over to their house I was anxious, but I knew God was with me. I truly didn't want to hurt my parents and cause them pain or sorrow, which was one of the reasons I kept this from them for 17 years. In addition, I was ashamed and didn't want them to be disappointed in me or think less of me. However, I was ready to tell them. I knew the Lord would be in the room with me holding my hand.

The one secret I kept, this one secret that the enemy had used to torment me, once brought into the light, became one of the most cherished, other worldly experiences I've ever had. When I sat down with my parents and told them what I had done 17 years earlier, they were both loving and kind.

However, there was something strange happening to my dad. As we sat there a glow overcame him. He was literally shining. As I spoke, he stopped me several times to stand and hug me. He sobbed when I asked him if I could give Aaron his last name. He said, "Yes, I want my grandson to have my name." Throughout this visit, in addition to his glow, he had a look of true anguish on his face. Somehow, I knew it wasn't because he was angry with me, but it was because he was hurt for me, for what I had gone through alone for 17 years. It was and still is the sweetest moment I've ever shared with him.

On the way home from telling my parents about my abortion, I was still in shock with my dad's behavior and this glow he had. I asked the Lord, "What was that all about?"

The Lord immediately told me, "I used your earthly father to show you how your Heavenly Father sees you." In that moment I cried and cried and thanked Him for loving me and forgiving me. I thanked Him for giving me this incredible gift. He came down and used my dad to show me the love of the Father. He turned my deepest, darkest, shameful secret into a miraculous event, displaying His glory, His forgiveness, His grace, His mercy and His love. Not only I will never forget, but I will treasure this truth forever.

When I think about how God knew us before He formed us in our mother's womb, I'm reminded of when He saved me at the age of seven. He knew when I was seven what I would do when I was 34—and He still saved me.

That is Grace! And because of His Grace I will forever walk in the freedom of His Forgiveness.

Angie Snellenberger is a wife to Dave, a mother to Zach and Shelby and the grandmother to Estabelle, Owen, Lucas and Reagan. She was raised in a Christian home, however found herself, as a single mom of two, pregnant and scared; she made the life-altering mistake of choosing abortion.

The years following her abortion she lived with denial, shame, depression and utter confusion. Seventeen years after her abortion, the Lord directed her to the SOAR (Spiritually Oriented Abortion Recovery) Bible study (Formally GRACE). By participating in this incredible Bible study, Angie found peace and with God's

help she began to walk in the freedom of God's miraculous forgiveness.

Currently, Angie is a co-facilitator with SOAR, and is humbled and honored to be able to have a front seat to witness God's amazing grace in transforming the lives of other post abortive women. She's also thankful for the other SOAR facilitators with whom she is honored to facilitate along side; they truly are her sisters in Christ and she loves them dearly.

Recently, the Lord orchestrated a change in Angie's world, enabling her to leave the corporate world behind and serve God at Life Centers in Indianapolis—ministering to women who are faced with an unplanned pregnancy, their precious babies and the community at large.

Outside of SOAR and Life Centers, Angie started a ladies group at her church called "For the Love of Babies". This group conducts a twice-yearly campaign in which baby items are collected from church members and all donations are given to clients of Life Centers. She  *spends her free time with her wonderful family, most notably her 4 little grandbabies who call her "Gigi" or "Juju" depending on which grand baby you ask!" These precious little ones are a testament to God's amazing Grace in her life and proof of the power of His mercy.*

Not Just Tissue

CHAPTER 6 • *Tara*

My name is Tara Lynn Broyles. I was born in Marion County, Indiana. I now live in very small town, Quincy, Indiana that may not be an actual, official town —it has only three roads.

I am a follower of Christ, a wife to a loving husband and mama to a daughter who is 24, a son that is 7-years-old, and a daughter that is 5-years-old!

Yes you read that correctly! I started all over in motherhood.

I was 18 when I became a mom to a precious baby girl, living the life of a teenage mama. That's a rough mama life, especially if you don't have a family that is capable of helping, which fortunately I did. Only God knows where I would be today if that were not my story.

My life had so much difficulty. I was mentally ill. I did drugs and booze. My baby's father was mentally ill and eventually would take his life a short time after Savannah was born.

It was a dark time, but she was the light. No matter what happened I had to keep living and attempting to be a better mama for her.

I was blessed 17 years later to be in a healthy stable relationship and become a mama to a sweet, adorable baby boy. Seventeen months later I was blessed with another daughter.

I am also the mama of a precious aborted baby boy.

When I think of him, he's always smiling and in the arms of Jesus.

Trusting Others, Not God

I was a child of God, but did not know nor understand what that meant. Many years later at the age of 33, I will understand what being a child of God means!

At the time of my abortion I was a mentally ill 16-year-old child, who was addicted to drugs. My role models were in the same situations as myself and I was raised in an ungodly home.

My family life was chaotic. My parents were going through a horrific divorce that dreadfully lasted for a few years.

I met a boy when I was 14 and I was convinced that I would spend my life with him. We both had our mental illnesses and used drugs. I was 16 when I started using cocaine. I was driving my younger brother home from school high on cocaine and crashed into a vehicle. Fortunately, nobody was hurt, but from the blood test that was drawn in the hospital, I found out that I was pregnant.

I had wanted to be a mom from the moment I could remember. The thought of having a tiny precious baby to kiss and snuggle was remarkable to me.

Pregnant? I sat on the hospital bed, staring at the person who delivered the news as if they were an alien. Of course I was having sex, but still, how am I pregnant? Of all the emotions pumping in my veins, the biggest emotion was fear. Fear becomes the strongest emotion; fear paralyzes you. All of my were reactions based on that fear.

With my recent information, combined with fear, I found myself sitting on my mom's bed in tears, telling her that I was pregnant. My mom was going through so much herself with three kids, a full time job, being recently separated from my father plus a divorce in the works.

She started to cry with me, and fear also filled her: fear of her child becoming a mom, fear of her child's father finding out she's with child, fear of her child's future. Her reactions came from that fear as well.

Unfortunately, no one in our household knew God. In that bedroom many moons ago, we came up with a plan to have an abortion: an abortion that would set God's fire in me many moons later. It was the beginning of the summer of 1995.

My boyfriend, my mom and myself set off to Planned Parenthood.

I was sitting in a black leather chair; I remember the texture and smell of it. When the doctor came into the office to confirm my pregnancy, I was numb. I don't remember the conversation much after hearing the words, "You are pregnant."

A few moments later, they are discussing whether or not I'm going to keep the pregnancy, give the baby up for adoption or have an abortion. The word "abortion" must have been said, because the word "baby" was never used again by any of the doctors.

I headed down the hall into the ultrasound room. During the ultrasound, I don't recall seeing the screen or ever being directed to look at it. I don't recall ever hearing a heartbeat.

I was told I was 12 weeks pregnant and that they could not do the abortion here. I would have to go to the Women's Center to have the tissue removed. Tissue???

Tissue... Tissue removed.... *Tissue..... You mean it's not a baby???*

Yes, the word "baby" had been replaced with the word "tissue" by these doctors. Tissue is how they referred to the baby, so who was I not to believe them? I trusted and believed in those words for about 19 years.

A few days later, I was in a cold room, lying on a table, having the "tissue" removed.

"You will feel some cramping," the doctor said.

The sound of the suction machine filled the room. I could feel the "tissue" being pulled from my uterus; it is a moment in time I will always remember.

I was given some pills to help with the discomfort and in 10 or so minutes, I was leaving the procedure room, heading home.

I trusted in the doctors. I trusted that when they called my baby tissue, it was the truth. I had absolutely no reason or cause to not trust them, they are doctors; intelligent, medical professionals. If they say my baby is tissue, then my baby must be tissue.

I do not remember the names or faces of the individuals that were involved in the actual abortion procedure. I don't know anything about them, except for the word "tissue" they expressed to me and the procedure they performed on me.

A procedure—that took just a few minutes—but would take 20 plus years to process.

In my soul at that time, I had little to zero emotion about this "tissue" that had been removed from my uterus. My life continued as if it had never happened. Two years later I became mama to a precious baby girl.

The Realization

During my three pregnancies, the only pregnancy that made me think of my aborted tissue was my last pregnancy. It was during an ultrasound when I was 12 or maybe 13 weeks pregnant. I was looking at the monitor as the tech was finding the baby and locating her heartbeat. As soon as I saw the image of my baby and heard the sound of her heartbeat, I became paralyzed. I couldn't breathe; I just stared. The tech was talking to me, but it was as if she were Charlie Brown's cartoon teacher. I could not understand a word she was saying.

All I could say was, "Please, do not take the baby off the screen yet." Her heartbeat sounded like it was coming through a megaphone and blasting through my body. The image of my baby on this monitor stopped my heart from beating. My ears were ringing. Her heartbeat was louder and louder, as if it was pulsating through my body.

I was staring at this image of a baby; a baby with a head, eyes, nose, mouth and ears. I could see her tiny face, her tiny body, her belly. She had ribs, arms, fingers; her legs were so long and her feet were fully formed. I could see that she was moving, and her heart was bouncing so fast in her chest. She was a tiny human being.

The word "tissue" screamed and vibrated through my body. This is not tissue!! This is a human being!! This baby is breathing!! She has a heart!! A heart!! She's alive!! She has functioning kidneys; she has tiny bones; her intestines have moved into her body.

Tissue!! This is Not Tissue!!!! That's a baby inside my uterus: a baby with a strong, beautiful heartbeat that is pulsating through my body.

Tears were flowing down my face and I was shaking. I was suddenly freezing. The tech had taken the ultrasound transducer off my belly. The sound of my baby's heartbeat could no longer be heard, but her heartbeat was still vibrating my body. The tech asked if I was okay and I just shook my head yes. She handed me the pictures of my baby. Eventually I was able to proceed home.

I don't understand why it took this particular ultrasound for my soul to realize that for 19 years, what I had believed and trusted from those doctors was not true! Anger reverberated through me as I held the pictures of my baby in my hands. The word "tissue" was screaming out of my pores!!!

How could those doctors lie?! How could they, as medical professionals, know that my baby had a heart, a head, arms, legs, tiny bones, a skull, that it was a baby and yet tell me that it wasn't a baby? They killed my baby!! I killed my baby!! I made the choice to kill my child!

Did the baby suffer? Of course it had to! Did somebody hold it as its heart quit beating? Was it just sucked up and left to die in that suction machine?!

All these emotions were raging inside of me, and there was absolutely nothing that I could do now. I wanted to find those doctors and beat them to prevent them from ever being able to tell others these lies!!

I cried for a very long time and had to push it all away to proceed with my life. I had no other choice.

I don't understand how I didn't at least realize this with my son's ultrasounds? We had 3D pictures done around the same time I did with this pregnancy. I saw the same images of him. I saw him sucking his thumb when he was 12-to-13 weeks old. I heard his heartbeat. I had more ultrasounds than normal with him, due to his size.

Yet I didn't have this realization until the ultrasound with her. I wonder: *How did I not see all this during his pregnancy?* I honestly cannot explain the reason.

Taken by Surprise

That would be my last pregnancy. I have three healthy, happy children. Praise God. My journey with God started when my youngest child was about eight months old. A year after I was baptized, I was signing up for church small groups when I noticed a group called SOAR (Spiritually Oriented Abortion Recovery). I thought that they'd probably just have a meeting where we could talk about our abortion, so I put my number on the sign-up sheet.

I began this group not expecting much, but thinking that we would gather around to discuss our abortions, trying to learn how to forgive ourselves and move on with our lives.

That's not at all what this group was. I had no idea what this group offered. This group was parents grieving for their aborted babies. The parents had attachments to their babies; these babies had names; and they were grieving over their abortions. They understood that they aborted human beings—not tissue.

I was still in denial, hiding behind the lies that my baby was tissue. I went to three group sessions. Each time I would leave, I felt drained and exhausted, as if I had been doing intense exercises. My body ached and would be sore for days.

There's a book that is part of this program. I despised the book! I would read a paragraph or two and slam the book down, throw the book across the room and scream at it as if it could understand me. I stomped on and punched this book.

I stopped going to the group. I couldn't mentally keep going. I had never thought about that aborted tissue as a baby, except for a short moment in time in the ultrasound room. But as a part of this group, you not only have to dig up your past and go back to those dark places you never want to revisit; you also have to dig and search for those chains. Those deeply embedded, dark, molded, disgusting, horrific, shameful chains, in order to analyze and rationalize those ugly truths, and bring them from darkness into the light.

I had vaulted those horrible dark chains away a long time ago and in my mind they were locked in that vault, never to be opened again. My soul fought the realization that I had actually murdered my precious baby so many moons ago and it wasn't going to accept that I did.

I didn't go back to that group. I threw all of the paperwork, including the book in the trash. I made sure that I took it out to the big trash bin, never to have to look at it again! I wasn't going back to the SOAR group, nor did I ever want to think about my abortion again.

Battling Chains

Another year went by. I found myself once again signing up for the group. Yes, the SOAR group. As soon as I signed up, I was angry. I didn't understand why I had signed up again. In my mind, my abortion was vaulted and that is where I wanted it to stay. *Why am I signing back up for this group? This is insanity!!*

But God... He knew these dark destructive molded, tangled, disgusting, horrific, ugly, shameful, anguished, bitter, horrible chains needed to be wrenched out of the dark, corroding vault that was locked in my soul. He brought it all out into His light so He could burst those chains out of my soul!

The process was brutal; the devil did not want me to be free from these horrific chains. The mental war for these chains to be brought into His light was raging. For the first time, I mentally had to replace the word "tissue" with the word "baby". My emotions were on fire. I wanted revenge; revenge for the doctors telling me that it was tissue! I wanted to tear their heads off. Yes, they lied, but I didn't protect myself or my child. I had to admit that I had murdered my child in that cold room many moons ago.

Through this group in which God placed me, I discovered how extremely important it is that all of our dark, shameful, terrifying, chains need to be battled. They need come into His light and be burst apart, so that we can live as we are supposed to live, free in Christ!

I had an incredible experience. My body began to shake. I could hear my heart pounding and the horrific vault that was bolted in my soul was being forced open. These dark molded, ugly, painful and shameful chains were being brought out to God's light and burst into pieces!!

I know this incredible amelioration. The first time that I felt God break one of my chains in Jesus's name, Jesus became my drug. Now, I chase Him. I will never get enough of God bursting all the chains that the devil used to bind me, keeping me from my freedom and joy in Christ. God bursting these chains in my body is Him telling me who I am in Him!!

Through this mental battle of breaking these chains free, God showed me that my baby was a boy. I could see his tiny body and his fingers that would have held mine so tight.

His name is Gage Allen Beauprez.

SOAR has a celebration of life for the aborted babies. This group is truly incredible. I encourage those who have had an abortion to go through this program and be set free!

I said his name for the first time out loud during the group's Celebration of Life for aborted babies, which is heartfelt, with so much love and kindness. You get to speak on your baby's behalf if you wish, and you're given a birth certificate—documentation of your precious baby. I never realized how important that documentation would be to me. It meant that my baby existed, that he wasn't just tissue. He was a tiny human being who is loved deeply.

To my precious Gage: *Mommy is so extremely sorry but blessed that you are a part of her life. I cannot wait until the day I get to stare upon your soul.*

Here's My Hope

If you do not have a relationship with God, I strongly encourage you to begin a relationship with Him. He will set you free, and by this freedom, you will have a joy inside that you will not even be able to explain! This freedom will let you love yourself and others as you're supposed to love and be loved. You will feel laughter in your soul.

I imagine the reason that most of the people who read this part of my journey is because they've had a similar journey. Maybe that is you.

I am so sorry for your loss, your guilt, your shame; but you are so loved. You may feel unloved or wonder, *How will someone ever love me after what I have done?* Or *How can I ever love myself?*

I say to you, "You are the love of Jesus' life! He died for you! Your baby is safe and is full of love and joy! You must find a way to forgive yourself so that you can feel love and joy like you have never felt before!" I encourage you to join an abortion group to help you process the death and life of your child.

If you are you are pregnant or may become pregnant and abortion is an option that you are considering or might consider, please understand that abortion might not feel like that big of an impact right now, but it will always be a huge impact on who you are and who you will be. This is a life or death decision.

I encourage you to always seek God's truth before seeking the truth from anyone else. I promise you it will save you from torturous chains in your soul.

Thank You, God!! Thank You, God!!!

God is Incredible!!

Always seek His truth from anyone else's truth!!!

Amen!! Amen!!

Tara and her husband, along with her three children, live in Indiana. Just a few years ago gave her life to Christ in 2018. Tara is living her life now for Jesus, the One whom she calls Lord and Savior, Healer and Deliverer!

You Were There

CHAPTER 7 • *Heather*

The day I killed my baby, I killed a part of myself that was lost forever. Or so I thought. I desperately desired healing and freedom from the guilt, shame and pain of the decision to abort my baby. This is my story of redemption.

Not Alone, Just Lonely

I grew up in mostly small towns in Illinois and Indiana. My parents divorced when I was five and I moved around a lot. My mom struggled for every dollar she brought home. As a single mother of three, she worked full time, leaving my older brother to help raise us. No amount of love and dedication from my mother could pay all the bills and keep enough food on the table.

When my dad refused to pay child support, my mom could no longer make ends meet. For the next several years, I bounced between my mother's and father's houses, occasionally spending a few months at my aunt's house. My relationship with my dad has always been strained. During periods of living at his house, it became more and more evident that he loved and valued his new wife and her daughters over me. I was a burden to him. Even in a house full of people, I felt isolated; alone and unwanted. Finally, my senior year, I moved back to my mom's hometown in northwest Indiana.

Although my mom talked about God, I grew up only knowing *of* Him, not knowing Him. We went to church on holidays, but I had no idea that a relationship with God existed or that He could fill the hole in my heart and remove the darkness from my life. I would later realize that only God could take away the shame, loneliness and worthlessness that was about to be heaped on my shoulders.

Drowning in Despair

I met my high school boyfriend at work. He was five years older than me and I was in love. I was naive to how badly he treated me until years later. Having very low self-esteem and unaware of my worth, I just knew I had finally found what I longed for as a child—I finally felt wanted. A couple of months before I turned 18, I found out that I was pregnant. I was panicked, but excited. I had wanted a baby since I was a little girl. I asked a friend to come with me to tell my boyfriend. He brought a friend with him, too. When I told him, he immediately demanded I have an abortion. I left the room in tears and could hear him laughing with his buddy, saying that he would push me down the stairs or kick me in the stomach—whatever he had to do to get rid of our baby. Although my world crashed in around me, I would've done anything not to lose him.

Devastated and confused by the decision made, I sunk into a deep stage of denial. Not wanting anyone to find out my secret, I waited until my 18th birthday to go to Planned Parenthood without a parental signature. I had to put what was about to happen out of my mind. I had to turn my emotions off before I could walk through those doors. Planned Parenthood made that easy—there was no counseling, no explanation of the procedure—the nurse even turned the monitor away from me so that I could not see the life growing inside of me. She turned the volume down so that I did not hear my baby's heartbeat. There was no choice; they took that from me.

Emotionally I was numb. They took me into the procedure room. It was so cold and lifeless. In my head, a voice kept saying, "Get up. Just get up." Instead, I just laid there, as still and as quiet as I could. The long metal rods and the noise of the vacuum were haunting. The pain was almost unbearable. I suppressed the screams that pushed to the surface.

Once the doctor was finished and I was out of the recovery room, my boyfriend took me out to eat like it was just a normal afternoon, he then dropped me off at my friend's house. I was flooded by guilt. I felt dirty and violated. I felt worthless. I wanted to stuff everything down and forget so that I wouldn't feel the pain of allowing someone to take my baby. The boyfriend that I would have done anything for was now a painful reminder of my abortion.

The aftermath of my abortion raged in cycles of guilt, shame, anger and depression. My behavior was unpredictable. I was spiraling out of control. I was drinking to the point of blacking out every weekend. I got arrested. I totaled three cars. I was in one relationship after the other and got engaged to four different men. I would be flooded with sadness out of nowhere. I was looking for something, anything—to fill this void. No matter how hard I searched, the darkness only deepened and the hole in my heart expanded at an alarming rate. I was looking in all the wrong places.

I was a mess. Why couldn't I have died on that table? What I went through was not simply a procedure, as I was told. It was life-altering, mind-numbing and spirit crushing. Why did no one tell me about the aftermath that would follow my choice? I was screaming for help, but no one could hear me.

Coming Up For Air

I went to a party two weeks after I broke up with my fourth fiancé and met Rob. He was handsome, sweet and kind, and he made me laugh. We started dating, fell in love and got married three months later. Our marriage was hard. I brought so much anger and resentment into it with me. My poor husband had to deal with my ugliness—my darkness.

We tried to have a baby right away. When we weren't getting pregnant, it made my depression worse. I cried out to Jesus, begging him, "Please Lord, please give me a child." I had been running from Him for so long and I was exhausted. I had very little faith that He would answer or that He loved me. I thought God was punishing me for my abortion and that I didn't deserve to be a mother. We had been married a year and I had never told anyone my secret, not even my husband. I finally got enough courage to tell him, just blurting it out. We never spoke of it again.

Over the next three years, we tried everything. We had fertility treatments. We tried fertility drugs. We tried one round of artificial insemination. I had a laparoscopic procedure and found out that I had endometriosis. The doctor said we had a three percent chance of ever getting pregnant. I just wanted it all to be over—my life, our marriage, everything. I felt hopeless. Thats when Rob and I decided to start researching adoption. We started the process. Five months later we were picked by a birth mom. Jackson Wade was born in July 2005. God saved my life when He allowed me to be the mother of this sweet baby boy.

I was happy, at least as happy as I ever thought I could be; as happy as I could be without healing. My life changed in a huge way when Jackson was born. I would do anything for him and for the first time in nine years, I cared about living. *Could God be done punishing me? Could He love me?* I knew that I wanted to raise Jackson in church, so we started attending with my family. We were still living in Northwest Indiana at that time.

My husband came to me one day and suggested we move to Indianapolis. *What?* I was not fond of this idea. My mom and most of our family lived nearby. This was my support network; these were the people I leaned into when I was struggling. However, moving was something Rob really wanted to do, so we talked about it. I reluctantly decided that if everything fell into place, then we would move to the Indianapolis area. The house sold sooner than we thought so off we went. We started looking for houses and found a beautiful home in a neighborhood full of kids. We decided to put in an offer, a really low offer, knowing it was a long shot. They turned us down, which we expected. Three months later, we got a call from the builders asking if we were still interested in purchasing the house at the price we had offered them. In amazement, we moved in shortly after.

Confronting the Source

We were still looking for a church and I was searching for volunteer positions while Jackson was at preschool. One day our neighbors, Diane and Bill, came by having mistakenly gotten a bill of ours in their mail. As we were talking and getting to know each other, they invited us to their church, Crossroads. I went that Sunday to check it out. As the pastor was preaching, I turned over the pamphlet to take notes and I saw it. It was a message from Life Centers, a crisis pregnancy center, and they were looking for volunteers. I thought, *This is perfect.* I felt connected to this church. I loved the pastor and the children's pastor.

We began attending as a family and that has been our church home now for over ten years.

The next morning, I called Life Centers and signed up for training. I had a plan: help enough women and it would atone for my sins. As I mentioned before, I didn't know God, so I didn't know that's not how He works. God's plan was better—much, much better.

On my third day of training, the director of the West Center, Machelle, shared her testimony about her abortion. Honestly, I was in utter disbelief that someone could so boldly talk about such a shameful memory. I wanted whatever it was that she had, but that was beyond terrifying to even think about. Then she dropped a bomb. Before being eligible to counsel at a center, anyone who has had an abortion had to go through GRACE. (GRACE was centered around Life Center's post-abortive Bible study, *Forgiven and Set Free*, by Linda Cochrane).

What?! Why does anyone need to know about the worst mistake of my life? I had carefully kept this secret for thirteen years and I certainly had no intentions of breaking that silence to a room of strangers. Before Machelle got out of the building, I was chasing after her. With tears in my eyes, not even being able to say the word abortion, I told her, "I'm fine. I just want to help other women." With a knowing look, Machelle assured me there was a class for me. Immediately the excuses began pouring out of my mouth.

Without hesitation she repeated, "Honey, we have a class for you."

I finished the training and reluctantly met Machelle to get my book for the Bible study. The class met the exact day and time that Jackson was in preschool. Unbelievable! I was angry that I had to go through this Bible study. I did not want to talk about my abortion. Besides, I was fine. I met with my facilitator's week after week. I fought it the whole time. I would hide in my bedroom doing my homework after everyone went to bed. My mom lived with us. I could not risk her finding out. I kept thinking I had to keep it together or I would not be able to volunteer.

When I read about the symptoms of post-abortive women and men, I thought, *That's me! That's why I'm depressed and angry. That's why I am so overprotective of Jackson. Why is this not talked about? Why is abortion glorified as a woman's choice when it is devastating and traumatizing? Abortion always takes the life of a child and sometimes the mother. Generations are changed.* I remember hearing this in GRACE: "You cannot take a life and not be affected in some way for the rest of your life."

My facilitators were amazing. Although I resisted and was beyond difficult as a student, I managed to make it through the entire study. The last day of GRACE we had a beautiful memorial for our babies. I didn't invite Rob. I was not ready to let him see this raw, vulnerable part of me. I have always regretted that decision. I had never allowed myself to grieve my baby. I never let myself think about my baby in the arms of Jesus. At the memorial, I felt the sweetness of my heavenly father. For the first time, I heard His whisper in my spirit, "Let go of the pain, my child. I'm strong enough to carry it. You don't have to live with those chains of bondage, my child. I will break them. Leave your guilt and shame at the Cross, my child. They have already been paid for." I broke. I could not stop sobbing. I had shoved it all down so far, for so long and fought to just get through each day for 13 years. I had kept this in the darkness, but no more. It was now in the light. I had been forgiven and set free.

Thank You, God, for pursuing me, never leaving me, never giving up on me. Thank You, God, for calling on Your people to come for me. Thank You, God, for cleansing me from all unrighteousness. Thank You, God, that as much as I fought You and turned from You, Your plan was better. You not only loved me, but You loved me so much that You created this elaborate plan to get me to Indianapolis to heal me of my abortion wound.

Slowly, I began to see the truths of His Word. God's love is unconditional, and no matter how many women I helped, it was not my good deeds that paid for my wrongdoing. Jesus paid that price. We are saved by grace through the blood of the Lamb and the word of our testimony.

Finally mentally and emotionally ready to begin volunteering at Life Centers, I was walking in my newfound freedom. God had cracked my protective walls. All of my anger and depression seeped out. Having been made new in Christ, I was saved that Sunday at church. He turned my heart of stone into a heart of flesh. I was on fire for the Lord and ready for the next step in my journey. I started volunteering with GRACE.

After three years of volunteering with the GRACE ministry, I witnessed firsthand God's perfect timing. Everything fell into place. Machelle asked me to speak at the upcoming memorial and Rob agreed to attend. I was finally ready to share this wounded part of myself with my husband. The night before the memorial God answered a special prayer—one that I had prayed so many times over the years. As I closed my eyes the image of a baby's feet wrapped in a pink blanket lingered in my mind. I was then given my baby's name: sweet Emma Mae. All of these elements aligned, giving me a precious gift from God, wrapped in the most beautiful package. With the knowledge of her name, I was genuinely able to mourn the loss of my baby, and gain another piece of God's healing power. In sharing my testimony and continuing to volunteer with GRACE, God teaches me something new each time. What an honor to be a hand in God's work.

Worth the Wait

Rob and I began another journey. With no hope of getting pregnant, we were building our family through adoption and felt blessed and excited. I continued to suffer with endometriosis, so I went to the doctor to discuss a hysterectomy. I wanted the physical pain to stop. My doctor agreed and said, "Yes. Your uterus has never done anything for you." I was still hesitant, but wanted to get on the schedule in the next couple of months. That was in July. On August 6th in a flurry of emotions we found out we were pregnant! We had been married for ten years. That is ten years of trying to conceive; ten years of doctors saying I wouldn't be able to get pregnant. I did not deserve to carry another baby, but the Lord is so sweet. Maxwell Cole was born in March of 2012. Our GRACE baby. Since when has impossible ever stopped God?

God continues to work in my life. He amazes me. Each step of the journey, God has shown His love for me, caring for every detail and providing me with a Godly support system.

Jackson was struggling with anxiety and kept getting misdiagnosed. God provided a friend for me—a confidant—a sister in Christ. I had spent days researching, crying and talking to doctors when Diane introduced me to a friend from church, Carrie. Carrie and her husband, Rick, are foster parents. They have one adopted daughter and two grown sons. Carrie was struggling with the same diagnosis for her daughter.

We joined Carrie and Rick's Life Group for adoptive and foster parents. Carrie and I became a support system for each other. Through women like Diane, Carrie and Machelle answering God's call, God made my life better than I would have dreamed to ask Him for. Times get hard and we have natural consequences of our sin, but God doesn't leave us there.

Breathing in God's Grace

Soon after that, Rob and I started fostering, but it wasn't good timing for our family. Our marriage was still in a rough spot. God was working on our hearts. There were hurt feelings and a lot of forgiveness that was still needed. I could not understand why our marriage wasn't mending along with the healing from my past, but God was working in our lives. I was now able to speak openly about my abortion as God led me. I shared my testimony in front of my church, my family and others. God surrounded us with strong, godly married couples, but ours remained broken. I cried out to God, "What am I doing wrong?!"

One afternoon, after Rob and I had been in a knock-down-drag-out fight, I was preparing to send him a text listing all the reasons I was still furious with him—about how I was right and he was so wrong. God said, "NO!" He brought me to my knees that day. Instead, I texted Rob, apologizing for my offenses—all of the things I had done wrong in our marriage. I sent him a list of good things; how he was a good man, sent to me by God, who stuck with me through all of the mess. God helped me see that my anger and guilt had been stealing the spotlight from our marriage. Ouch! It isn't always easy to look inward, but the pain it causes is always worth it if you put in the work. In 2019, we renewed our vows, putting God in the center of our marriage. In October 2022 we will celebrate 20 years.

As soon as we returned from our marriage renewal, we started the process of renewing our foster license. We have fostered a few children since then. Carrie and I were having lunch one afternoon when she got a call from the Indiana Department of Child Services needing a home for a drug addicted baby. The little girl had just been born. With three foster kids already, Carrie handed me the phone. We had our boys plus two foster children at the time. *Am I crazy?* I called Rob and asked him about taking this baby girl. He said yes!

A few days later I held this precious baby in my arms. After two years her adoption became official. Emerson Wren was born in August of 2019. What if Carrie had not listened to Jesus that day at lunch? We love our baby girl, an oh-so-perfect surprise from my heavenly Father.

Always There—Never Alone

Reflecting on the path I took, I realize that through the darkness and pain in the aftermath of my abortion, God was there, fighting for me. Even through my destructive behavior while trying to escape my shame and guilt, God was there protecting me from myself. Through the struggles of infertility, adoption and an unsteady marriage, God was

there growing my understanding and my character. Even on the operating table at the abortion clinic, God was there whispering, "Get up. Just get up." I merely had to learn to listen to that still, small voice. In the loneliness, in the celebrations, in the pain and in the healing, I was never alone. God, You were there.

All of these steps prepared and led me to where I am now—with a healthy marriage, three healthy children and the empathy and experience to help other women come out of the darkness and walk in freedom. The part of me that I thought I had lost so many years ago at that abortion clinic turned out to be a building block for God making me who I am today. There is no limit to what God can do in our lives, turning ashes to beauty. He is always there.

Heather Wilson is a wife, mom, foster mom, author and servant to the Lord. Heather recently started a small Christ-Centered t-shirt business, Redeemed by Design. *With two sons and the adoption of her baby girl final, her heart is overflowing with love. Heather loves Jesus, her family and friends. She is in awe of God's reckless love and ability to heal the bound-up and broken-hearted.*

After getting married and adopting her now teenage son, she never had to think twice about leaving the workforce and staying home to raise their children. Becoming a foster parent was just one way she could love on babies without filling her home with more little toes than her husband could count. She loves seeing God do his thing in the SOAR ministry (Spiritually Oriented Abortion Recovery), where she has helped facilitate the post-abortive Bible study since 2011.

When The Lord broke Heather's chains by healing her from the pain, guilt and shame of her abortion, he put a fire in her and a passion for helping women find healing, speaking out for the voiceless and helping children find the love they deserve.

A Rough Start

CHAPTER 8 • *Lisa*

The first memory I have as a child is a nightmare. I always woke up to the same nightmare, a baby doll with red eyes just falling through dark space. The first memory I have of my mother is when she brushed the hair off my forehead while I was feverish. I was in bed. She woke me up and I could smell the alcohol on her breath; but that is the only recollection of her showing affection that I could honestly pull from memory. I don't remember much at all until I was five when my mother married for the fifth time to my last step-father. She and he walked through the door and said, "We're married!" I remember shock then anger. I didn't like this man at all. Alcoholism and drug addiction ruled our house. I had two older siblings, ten and seven years older. Later I had a younger sister by the step-father. We were all from different marriages.

The Nightmare Continues

My life-course was driven by addiction's timeline and my family was a swirling tornado of survival of the fittest. Looking back it was confusing, because I remember times when my mother was the Girl Scout leader and the PTO President, yet she showed up drunk to pick me up or embarrassed me in some way. I learned to survive by keeping my mouth shut and isolating in the safe haven of my room at home. I never knew what would happen when I walked in the door from school. It is a history of being dismissed and abandoned.

I had a father involved every other weekend. I know he tried, but his marriage to my stepmother and her abusive children didn't help. I didn't know until years later through therapy that I was being sexually molested by a stepbrother. Growing up, sexuality was not talked about. I was taught to close my eyes if sexual scenes came across the screen at movies or on TV shows. I learned about sex from school and friends. I was grossly misled and immature, so much so that when I was molested at 13, I thought that the 18-year-old molesting me was my first boyfriend and I was in love. Thankfully my mother stepped in and stopped that one before I was raped.

My reputation at school was obliterated. I was humiliated by rumors and mean teenagers. I was just so angry all the time. The first time I tried to commit suicide was at 15. I didn't know how to deal with the pain from any part of my life; I felt crazy, angry, fragmented. I had no idea my anger was PTSD from my childhood and I didn't know how to deal with my emotions, let alone grow up. I'd never been taught. I lived in constant emotion, constant survival mode. My only goal was one day to get out of the house, thought I didn't know how that would happen.

I started my downward spiral into addiction at age 15 or 16. That coincided with sexual promiscuity and my first (in my mind) real boyfriend, who I thought would be my "high school sweetheart". I am the one who pushed for sex at 15 when I was in no way ready for it. My friend's mother—not my mother—talked to me about sex and took me to the local Planned Parenthood. In fact, my mother didn't know at all. My friend's mother made the appointment for me, signed the paperwork and I walked out within a few hours with birth control. A hormone to regulate my reproductive system at 15-years-old, without a parent's permission, even back in 1985-86. Needless to say, the relationship with my "high school sweetheart" didn't last, but it set up my sexual promiscuity and a pattern of trading out my body for what I thought was love in future years. My childhood experiences of being groomed by older men, sexual molestation and childhood trauma set a course for self-destruction.

I became pregnant the first time at 19. The first thought that went through my mind was: *Get an abortion.* I went to a free clinic and the doctor confirmed my pregnancy. He looked at me and asked, "Is this a happy moment or not?"

I said, "No it's not." I was shocked to be pregnant because I had been told earlier that because of a pelvic inflammatory infection, I would not be able to get pregnant. Yet there I was, pregnant. I was in between relationships. My boyfriend and I had just broken up. I was starting to feel better about myself after that bad relationship. When the first word that popped into my mind was abortion, I didn't even think about keeping it. I told the father. We both agreed to have an abortion and we split the cost like we would have a dinner bill, I write with grief.

I made the appointment at a local clinic. Walking up to the door that morning I saw women holding signs of aborted babies, so I pretty much ran inside so as not to see them. It was one of the most depressing, sad days of my life. I sat in the waiting room, then was ushered back into a room for an ultrasound. I wasn't allowed to look at the screen but I found myself wanting to. I was eight weeks along, meaning my price would not be as high, as they initially believed I was 10-weeks along. Imagine, a sales process on abortions. When the nurse took me back to the suction room, I was already uncomfortable because I did not like pelvic exams. I kept questioning myself: *Why I was there; how I could do this?* But then the thought came to not worry: *It wasn't really a baby anyway.* The procedure started. I was holding on to the nurse's hands so tightly as she kept saying, "If you don't really want this, then why are you here?" I was just angry at her and the doctor who kept telling me to relax; he was almost jovial. I just wanted to punch him, but I hated myself immediately.

The painful abortion was over in a few minutes and I was shell-shocked. I felt like a part of me had died. The nurse escorted me out to this room where a TV was playing amid a circle of recliners. I sat there in a room full of quiet, recovering women. It was just pathetic. My heart was broken and I didn't know why. I left that day feeling like a part of me had died. That's the only thought that I had in my head. Realistically, without my knowing yet, a part of me DID die. My baby had died.

Battling to Wake Up

A few months later, I was back with the ex-boyfriend and ended up pregnant again, this time in June. I later learned that over 50% of women who have an abortion end up pregnant again within six months. That was me—pregnant again. At first I thought of another abortion, but my child's father said, "No, we can do this. We can do this." Another point I have learned in post-abortive recovery is that the father is also a huge part in the deciding factor for a woman to keep her child. I kept my baby. By the fifth month of pregnancy, the father was back to his old antics. I had caught my child's father with his ex-girlfriend. I was betrayed again and left feeling isolated and alone.

I couldn't live that way and I was desperate to get out of our relationship. I opened the phone book (there were no cell phones back then) looking for the word, "abortion". Instead I found the word, "adoption". Thanks be to God.

I know this was God's hand moving my finger to the word adoption. I was almost five to six months pregnant. I was desperate just to not be pregnant because of the emotional pain that I didn't know how to cope with. I had this baby inside me that I could not do anything about and didn't know how to care for.

I went to Bethany Christian Centers, which was a local adoption agency. The center was closed, but thankfully, a woman met with me at 9:00 AM the day after Thanksgiving. She prayed with me. She helped me by asking me questions and counseled me towards keeping my baby. She explained what adoption meant for my child and myself. The next few months were horrendous. I went back and forth between the ideas of parenting my child or giving her up for adoption. I was being counseled towards parenting while preparing financially for being a mother, but I was also being counseled that adoption was still a choice.

The state laws were different then and my daughter's father would not sign the papers to give her up for adoption before my daughter's birth. He supposedly still wanted to parent her; he just didn't want to do it with me. I did not want my daughter to grow up in a single home like I did, but through it all, I chose to parent after my daughter was born. The moment she was born I erupted in a love for another human being I'd never known. She was precious and sweet and smelled so good, like a sweet baby. My baby.

In the beginning, parenting was just so hard. Nothing instinctual inside of me prepared me for parenting. I was a good mom; I did the things I was supposed to do, or so I thought, yet something inside just felt broken. I found out much later it had to do with my unhealed emotional afflictions and that I had absolutely no relationship with God. I would pray and get so close, but I had no intimacy with God; it was more of a fear. I read parenting magazines. I went to counselors for help. I did receive counseling from the counselor at the adoption agency (above and beyond her duties, I assure you) to help me emotionally parent. It worked for a while.

My alcoholism was starting to pick up when my daughter was four. On one hand, I was going back to school, doing everything that I should and I was parenting. I had this beautiful little girl, but on the inside of me, I was thinking, *What is wrong with me?* That was my addiction speaking. It was telling me that it would come before my child. I was in between relationships with men, trying to look for an idealistic marriage to make a family, for which I had no reference. It wasn't good for her, for me or for anybody involved. I found myself pregnant again within a few years of my daughter's birth, even after taking precautions not to get pregnant. Immediately I had an abortion. My first thoughts were all the familiar lies that Satan puts in the thoughts of women who are in crisis pregnancy: *I'm already a single mother. I can't afford another child. It's not fair to my daughter.*

By my late 20's into my early 30's, I was involved with two different men and became pregnant by each of them. Sadly, I went to the same abortion clinic as I had for the previous pregnancies. By the fourth abortion, as I was squirming and in pain, the same doctor said, "Huh! After four abortions, you should be used to this." My heart was so broken. I was in the depths of alcoholism and drug addiction, not knowing what to do. I wanted better for my daughter than this pathetic life. I was struggling and broken. Unhealed people cannot produce nor facilitate healthy relationships.

When I was 35, spiritually bankrupt and almost homeless, I lost custody of my daughter. I went to an AA meeting and ended up talking with a woman after the meeting who got my phone number and information. That night she and another recovering alcoholic came over to my house and "12-stepped" me, which means they talked to me about my alcoholism and addiction. I told them that I didn't know how to live with alcohol or without alcohol and she said, "I can show you."

My daughter's father had gotten married and my daughter was being raised by them, thankfully. I had no business being a parent and my daughter had no business being raised in my situation. By the time I was three years sober, a lot of my anger and pain started coming out in outbursts.

Coming Out of the Dark

My outbursts of anger seemed to coincide with a woman's pregnancy, who at the time, was in the same home group with me. It was suggested, that because of my unresolved anger, that I seek help about the multiple abortions I experienced. I had never made the connection that the abortions could affect me so deeply emotionally and spiritually. I never understood that abortion could be traumatic. I happened to search on Google for a post-abortive recovery program and there was one right around the corner from my work, which in hindsight, I knew to be God's grace. To search for help, to find it not only right around the corner, but also to have a session starting within a week? Only God Himself could coordinate this.

I learned about GRACE Ministries—what became the SOAR program (Spiritually Oriented Abortion Recovery), and made an initial counseling appointment with Machelle Montgomery. I walked into her west side office for my appointment, sat down and was immediately overcome with a gentle, safe, nudge (I'm sure the Spirit). I emotionally purged my story. Her eyes were the most compassionate I've experienced. It wasn't pity—it was compassion she gave me. She started asking me questions about my abortion experience. I told her my story, about each abortion, and she told me about post-abortive syndrome (PAS). I was starting to believe in God really for the first time I could recall, through my recovery and now through experiencing God's grace.

I was starting to believe that addiction had killed my children. I was starting to believe that I could stay sober. I was starting to believe I could live a different life. I had hope for the first time in my life that my unceasing anger and spiritual pain could be explained. I attended post-abortive counseling, a *Forgiven and Set Free* class and then a retreat for the healing of women and men who have experienced the pain of abortion. It was a beginning to my healing. I had the opportunity to name my children; they received birth certificates; I learned to pray for them and to see them as children. The therapeutic value of sitting in a room full of women sharing their post-abortive stories illustrated how Christ redeemed all of our pain to help others heal. Only God could do this.

Awake and Alive

Through sobriety, a healing began. It started with an acknowledgment of God's grace and then grew into a longing for God, I believe through the healing of my abortions. My spiritual father at the time, the very Reverend Fr. Nabil Hanna, explained that my baptism into the church is only the beginning of a journey with God. It has been that and more. Through the sacraments of the church, I began another journey and salvation by experiencing God's hand in my post-abortive healing. Even after the first SOAR retreat, looking back, I can see that I still did not believe that I was forgiven but believed that God had my children with Him. Unknowingly, I still had a deep self-loathing. The Orthodox faith, patient and loving spiritual fathers, and a lot of counseling and work have paved a very painful, but loving and healing path for me.

It is a miracle that I have gone from full feminist and leftist liberal, not believing that a "clump of cells" was a child to fully believing that pregnancy begins at conception and is a gift from God. I learned through my spiritual fathers in the Orthodox Church, SOAR, and sobriety that addiction required me to murder my children. Through the sacraments, I was learning to take responsibility for the weight of the sin and then let God take the burdens as He lovingly does.

God continually redeems me through post-abortive recovery and in sobriety, by helping other women. I was told that my story would one day help women, and years later I sat across the table from a woman who, for the first time, spoke about the abortion that she'd been forced to have years ago. The pain that she was in pulled mine out to reveal

God's grace and He used my experience to help another woman! He lifted me up in joy in that tearful moment so that I could say, "Me, too."

I've stayed in contact with Machelle Montgomery through the years of my recovery and spiritual growth. When I was about 10 years sober, I asked about possibly becoming a volunteer through SOAR. Machelle recommended that I take SOAR again—this time as a retreat. The program had changed so much in 10 years, with the inclusion of the book, *Forgiven and Set Free*.

I attended it, but this time I was in a different emotional place as I had been seeing a spiritual counselor to help me work through my childhood trauma. This time I experienced the study from a completely different perspective, which is what God's healing does.

My love for post-abortive recovery has grown so much that I want to start a ministry like this in the Orthodox Church. We do not have one yet, but through Orthodox Christians for Life, a start has been made. We are very far behind our brothers and sisters in the Catholic and Protestant churches, who not only talk about the pro-life movement, but live it out and talk about abortion openly. The devastation and the culture of murder has traumatized so many women, men, children and families. This insight led me to the next layer in the healing process.

Almost immediately after experiencing SOAR for a second time, and the joy of stepping further into God's grace and forgiveness, I was able to experience a post-abortive retreat through the sacraments in the Catholic Church at Rachel's Vineyard. I was upfront with facilitators, letting them know that I am Orthodox, but that I was longing to see the differences between Protestant and Catholic retreats. I had one spiritual experience, if not a few, at Rachel's Vineyard. Even after doing the work for years through other post-abortive retreats, for the first time that I could remember, I *knew* I'd been set free and forgiven by God and I forgave myself. His timing is always perfect. I could close my eyes and see my children: Matthew, Connor, John, and Paul, with their Heavenly Father, safe and happy. One day, I pray, I will see them. My experience at Rachel's Vineyard, coupled with my counseling, gave me a closure; forgiveness and healing that needed to happen.

The truth is, it is ongoing. I think about my children and often I pray for them, lighting candles weekly before I enter liturgy. The Orthodox faith has taught me well to pray for their souls and I know that Christ has my children. I have much joy in knowing this. My heart has yearned for a post-abortive recovery program and retreat within the Orthodox faith, and I've been working with Emily Wilkinson off and on for years through Orthodox Christians for Life (OCLife) to achieve this. The conversations about abortion are still uncomfortable for many. Many other organizations such as Right to Life and Life Centers are established and have experience with it. One day, I pray to help women within the Orthodox Church come to see that there is hope and healing from the pain and grief of abortion. I think the church forgets sometimes that so many of us are converts.

I enjoy the 40 Days for Life Campaign each year. We pray as a group, whether it be with OCLife, or with my Catholic friends, reciting the Rachel's Rosary.

Last year God opened my eyes and heart to visualize how Christ must have been with me in those cold, sterile, murderous rooms. While I was getting the abortions He was crying for me, when I didn't know how to cry for myself—yet. He received my children immediately.

I believe that when we pray to the Theotokos (Mary, Christ's mother) she comes running immediately. Who else, but the most compassionate of Mother's, could suffer with us as we grieve our children? I know she is with me and at every grave site called Planned Parenthood.

My daughter is close to 30 now and we have quite a road to go with our own healing. Sometimes I look at her and I can imagine her four brothers that she doesn't even know. We haven't discussed all her siblings. Abortion is a painful topic, and she is exactly who I was at that age. There is hope though, always. I've been sober for 15 years and have been in counseling for the past few years to help me deal with the trauma, so that I can move forward. God illustrates in my life how He continues to love me by providing a loving man. I am engaged to be married in January 2022. What timing? The anniversary of Roe v. Wade.

I pray that my story helps women recover from a hopeless state of mind and being, and then be able to receive healing of body and soul. I pray my story resonates with you, and that you can experience a loving and redeeming God through my eyes. For surely, my life has been ransomed for others to see hope in healing.

The End is Just the Beginning

Chapter 9 • Danielle

shouldn't have been there for more than a couple of hours, but two hours slowly turned to six hours. Simon had to leave to pick up our daughter, so I waited alone. When I walked out of the clinic and got into the car, where he'd been waiting, I saw our 10-month-old baby girl sleeping peacefully in her car seat, unaware of what I'd just done. I closed the door of the car and we drove away. I had every intention of leaving that day behind those metal gates protected by locks. My secret would stay there along with all the others on that day.

In the days, months, and years after my abortion, I was fighting an internal battle. I tried to convince myself that it was just a procedure. That maybe I was going to have a miscarriage anyway. I tried to convince myself that it wasn't a big deal. The denial quickly turned into pleading with God to forgive me—to save me from what I'd done. How could He forgive me? Why would He forgive me? I hated myself for what I'd done. It became hard to live in my skin. I wanted to crawl outside of my body because living inside of myself felt like torture. There came a point that I didn't want to live anymore.

A Haunting Past

We already had a baby. I couldn't have two babies. We weren't married and I was so afraid of being a single mom to two kids. What if he didn't stay? What if he didn't want to be a dad? My family legacy haunted me and I feared history repeating itself.

My mom was a single mom. Two of my aunts were single moms. It felt like a curse on our family that we could have children but we couldn't seem to keep the fathers of our children. I already felt the judgment of having one child without being married and feared the humiliation of having yet another child and not being married. He loved me. He loved our daughter; but he had absolutely no reason to stay.

My own childhood had taught me that men didn't have an obligation to care for their children, emotionally, spiritually, or financially. My expectations were low and my decisions were ruled by fear. My dad had made the decision not to parent or participate in my life and I was prepared for my child to have the same experience. It's hard to grow up not knowing that you are loved by your dad. To know that there are other more important things than caring for you. There is a sense of worthlessness that comes with the abandonment that an absent father leaves behind. I could help my daughter navigate life without a dad, but it would be so much harder to do with two kids.

Simon didn't leave. We got engaged the day before our daughter turned one! We got married a year later. I thought that once the vows were exchanged and rings were on, all the mistakes would just disappear. I thought that I'd finally be able to live and that marriage would fix all my brokenness. Well, that's not how marriage works. Two very broken people do not make the sum of one whole, they just live broken together. I felt so much shame in our marriage that freedom felt impossible. All of that baggage, all of those years of being in and out of abusive relationships, all the drug and alcohol abuse did not fall away. It followed me into our home.

I had grown up in church. I had been baptized in the church, but I was very far from God. After becoming a mom I had the nagging feeling that if I didn't do anything else well for my daughter that the least I could do was give her the opportunity to meet Jesus. After we were married, some friends invited us to try a church with them. We went and we still call that church our home. I had been able to hide my secrets from people, from family, and from friends, but when I sat in church I couldn't hide from God. I would try to conceal my weeping heart and my tears from other people. I was an impostor and I didn't want to be exposed. Living in a web of lies and secrecy was more than I could bear.

Hiding from my mom was one of the hardest parts of my post-abortion experience. I had told my aunt, her sister just days after my abortion. My aunt promised not to tell my mom. We were close but I didn't want to disappoint her. I was so afraid of letting her down; of her being ashamed of me. Every time I was with her I felt like I was lying by not telling her. So many times I would start to spill the words and I'd quickly shut it down. I didn't know if I'd ever muster up the courage to tell her.

After Simon and I were married we wanted to add to our family. I knew I was capable of getting pregnant. We'd had one miscarriage, one living child and one abortion, but I couldn't seem to get pregnant.

Other women would comment on the second baby being the hardest to get conceive, but they didn't know my story. To them, I only had one child but in reality, I'd already had three pregnancies. My guilt and shame was accompanied by anger and fear. *God must be punishing me*, I thought. He didn't trust us with another baby. He'd given us that chance and we gave our baby back. We sent her away, unwanted. Why would He trust us now?

After two years of trying combined with hormone replacement therapy, I got pregnant. This was what we'd waited and prayed for. Another baby girl was born and everything seemed right in the world. God had answered our prayers. What I didn't know was that the experience of having a new baby would lead me back to that clinic, back to that table, and a new battle that I'd have to fight through.

Grace Abounds

After our baby girl June was born, the guilt and shame became crushing. What appeared to some as postpartum depression was the past showing up to be reckoned with. Our baby girl was a year old and the depression was thicker than I'd ever experienced. I knew depression like an old friend that would come to pay a dreaded visit. I could sense when she was near. We'd hunker down together and I'd wait for the time of exit. I'd be relieved when she'd go away and dread her return, not knowing when that time might come. This time the exit seemed to be never. She was not interested in showing herself out the door.

My unhappiness was palpable. One day, Simon looked at me and asked, "Can you just pretend to be happy for a little while?" My disdain was making everyone around me miserable, including our children.

I began to cry. "I don't know how to be happy!"

I was putting our five-year-old daughter, Mabel, to bed one night when she asked, "Why don't you love me?" It absolutely wrecked me. One of my greatest fears had come true. I knew what it felt like to not be loved and I never wanted my child to know that pain. I lived with her. I took care of her, but I could not show her that I loved her. I had failed her. I needed help but didn't know where to go.

At my lowest, I Googled 'abortion support group'. Life Centers was the first one to pop up. I emailed the contact for the support group, Machelle. I fully expected her to be cold and judgmental but her kind smile and joyful spirit put me at ease. She helped me into a class, SOAR, where I would get the help I so desperately needed. I just wanted a safe space to say out loud that I'd had an abortion. I didn't know that healing from my abortion was even a possibility. I thought that I would at least learn how to cope with the shame and guilt if this was the life I was destined to live.

Before starting the class I gathered the courage to tell my mom. I needed people in my corner as knew this would be a battle and I knew she could and would help me. With tears in her eyes she hugged me. "I wondered," she said. "I thought something must have happened because you cry every time we're in church." Mom didn't run away. She held on tighter.

Working through every part of my abortion experience felt like bringing up a new painful piece. It was all hard. Nothing about it felt easy, but I'd never in my life experienced the nearness of Jesus until I was in that space. I felt Him sitting next to me while I wept for my baby. While I mourned over a past that had left me a shell of a person. He was there. Though painful for me, He was gentle. I knew it would be hard but I also knew that my life and the well-being of my family depended on my healing. I would never be able to be a good mom if I stayed in the place where I was emotionally. I couldn't be a good wife and I didn't think our marriage would survive if I didn't give this up. I'm so thankful He doesn't leave us where we are when we finally surrender to Him.

Simon wasn't ready to work through it with me, but I knew I had to keep pushing forward. I wasn't angry with him, but I needed him. I had made the decision to have an abortion and he followed my lead, but our relationship needed healing from that choice. Forgiveness needed to happen; apologies needed to be exchanged; but even without him working through it with me, I felt the intimacy of my loving Father. That was what I needed. I needed to feel the warmth and acceptance of a loving Dad that would hold me in spite of my choices. Simon would follow, but it had to start with me. As a mother, I couldn't end the life of my child without suffering the intense repercussions of having my baby aborted from my womb. I took complete ownership of the choice to abort my baby and I had to work through it, one on one, with God.

The deeper I got into my healing, the more God would reveal to me. When I was ready, He would place something gently before me to grieve then mourn and accept. I woke up one night from a nightmare. It startled me and sat me up in our bed in disbelief. I had been lying on an exam table, my shirt pulled up and pants down low. A lady with an ultrasound wand ran the machine across the goo on my belly. She asked, "Do you want to hear the heartbeat?"

"No!" I replied. And I woke up confused and disoriented. Why would I do that? I was disgusted with my dreaming self. When I'd been pregnant with Mabel and June, hearing their heartbeat was everything. It gave me relief that they were well and growing snuggly inside me.

Immediately I was thrown back into the reality that this scenario wasn't a dream—it was a memory. Minutes before my abortion I lay in a dark room with a tech asking if I wanted to hear the heartbeat and letting me know that I was seven and a half weeks pregnant. I had refused to accept that it was a baby. It was a fetus, and I wanted nothing to do with it. I will always have regret. There isn't a day that passes that I don't regret taking the life of my daughter. Simultaneously, I can walk in freedom knowing that I am forgiven and our gracious heavenly Father is caring for my daughter.

All Your Promises are Yes and Amen

I have an image of my little girl. Her name is Iris Noel. I think she's probably four or five. She looks a lot like my daughter Pearl. She has brown wavy hair that bounces when she runs, thick, chubby legs in a pair of purple shorts, and a yellow t-shirt with ruffles hugging her pudgy belly. My heart aches to grab her, hold her and kiss her squishy cheeks. She wasn't real to me when I decided to have an abortion, but she's real to me now. Going through SOAR gave me the opportunity to mourn her—to give her the dignity she deserves—to be given a name and a face.

Simon went with me to the memorial service where I said, "Hello" and "Goodbye". Walking through the healing process of my abortion has been nothing short of God's goodness and kindness. He's given me such a gift to mourn her life while allowing me to live mine out abundantly. Sometimes it feels so unfair that I am allowed to reap the benefits of His grace, but we go on for the living. We are given healing to help heal others. The abortion of my child will not be in vain. I've been given the gift to walk through this process with other women and to mourn with them. These women are like sisters to me. We share a kind of loss not known by others. None of us wants to be a part of this secret society of loss, but in our pain and need, God gave us each other to love and encourage and hold up our hands to the sky when worship feels impossible. He is good. He is good. He is so very good!

My mom didn't come to my memorial, but when I facilitated one of the classes, I invited her to come. She was thankful for the invitation and went with me. It changed her. It opened her up to something she'd not understood and she felt called to be a part of it. She helps with memorials now and loves being involved. It's been such a blessing to have her on this journey with me. Her love and kindness to all of us that have had abortions is an example of the love and kindness of Jesus. She will do the work so that we can walk a little easier through the murky waters. Why did I ever think she would be less than supportive? Because that's what living in secrecy does. It convinces us that we are not worth love and acceptance, but Jesus will reach down and put the very people that we need in front of us, even the very people we fear will walk away.

My daughter Mabel is 14 now. Iris would be 12 and a half. There have been times where I look at Mabel and wish with all my heart I'd not taken her sister away from her. I remember sitting at a soccer game with her one evening and seeing friends of hers with their sisters. Knowing that her sister was missing brought me to tears. They might have been great friends. We'll never know. We will apologize to our children for taking the life of a sibling that would have been a blessing and dearly loved in our family.

June is nine now. I tell my daughters every day that I love them. I want nothing more than for them to know that I love them with every ounce of my being. As a mom, I've been able to give them all of me. I pour my heart into my kids. Had I not gone through SOAR, I don't know that would have been possible.

God gave us another daughter, Pearl, and she *is* a pearl. She brought so much healing into our family. I found out that I was pregnant with her two days before the anniversary of having my abortion. She was born in February, likely when Iris would have been born. When Pearl was born, she had a line that ran through the Iris of her eye, and we believed it was a reminder of God's redemption story in our life.

Then we were blessed with a little boy named Otto. When I look back at the punishment that I thought God was heaping upon me, I wonder if I'd be able to parent Otto without guilt and shame. He was born with Arthrogryposis Mulitplex Congenita, a physical disability. If I hadn't gone through the healing process, would I think that Otto's condition was my fault? Would I think it was another form of punishment? I don't know. I think that I might have thought that this was something I brought upon my child: my son paying for the sins of his mother. Instead, I look at him and only see God's abundant love in my life. God keeps showing Simon and me just how wonderful He is, how abundant His love is for us. All those years ago when we met in a college bar, God was putting together a story that has led us to today.

Would I have made it through without the healing of God? The path of destruction I was on says possibly not, but He didn't leave me where He found me. He has allowed Simon and me to share our story. Our marriage is a testament to God and God alone. We wouldn't have made it through all that we have without Him, and we're stronger on the other end. We met as two very messy people who only created more mess, but God took our mess and is making a masterpiece.

There will always be trials but we can stand with confidence in the love of God, knowing that there's not a storm we can't weather. He's always been next to me even when I couldn't see Him. He's blessed our marriage and guided us through. Simon has been the hands and feet of Jesus in our marriage. God has given Simon a strength and patience that I didn't know existed. He's given us four beautiful children that teach me daily about the love of Jesus. How kind He has been. We just need to trust Him and allow Him to do the work of redemption in our lives.

He'll do it if we allow Him. Blessings!

Being a Single Mother

DANIELLE'S MOTHER · Mary

I always wanted to get married and be a mom. I got married on my 21st birthday and thought my dreams had come true. My white picket fence life was beginning; I was a wife, and would someday be a mother to four children who would have a life and home filled with love and endless bliss. However, that was not to be. Within a matter of weeks it began to fall apart: he was an addict. Believing that my love would change him, I stayed.

Jesus was with me. We sought counsel with our parish priest and around nine months into our marriage, he suggested that we attend a retreat. At that retreat we met people that became dear friends and were a pivotal part of my journey. They prayed with us, loved and supported us and truly were the hands and feet of Jesus.

Two years into our marriage, I gave birth to a beautiful baby girl that we named Danielle. I was so full of love for her and overwhelmed that God had entrusted me with this child. There wasn't anything that I wanted more than to be a good mother, and I knew I needed His help. I prayed every day that God would help me to be the mother He wanted me to be.

The addiction was bigger than my husband. When Danielle was a year old we divorced and he took off. I do want to say this before I go on; the addiction was bigger than him, but it wasn't bigger than God. My husband wasn't willing to accept the healing that I know God had for him.

I never wanted to be divorced and I didn't want my daughter to be the stereotypical child of divorce—scarred for life. I was afraid. I was afraid my daughter would be wounded by the absence of her father. I was afraid I wouldn't be enough for her. I was afraid I wouldn't be able to provide for her. I had nothing more than a high school diploma. No marketable skills that would provide the income needed to raise a child, but Jesus was with me. A wise, godly man told me to tell Danielle every day that I love her. He said as long as children know they're loved they'll be okay. I followed his advice. Jesus is our provider and He provided me with an 8:00 AM to 5:00 PM job for 40 hours a week. In fact, I worked there for over 30 years.

I was raised Catholic and Danielle and I went to Mass every Sunday. Jesus was with me and continued to move. Through a series of circumstances He put a woman named Penny into our life. She invited us to her church and we eventually became members of First Baptist Church. Again, Jesus placed us in a community of people that taught us more of His word and His truth. They loved us well and they too were the hands and feet of Jesus to us.

I want to be honest. It wasn't always easy but Jesus was with us every step of the way. I was not a perfect mother but Danielle always knew how much she was loved. Money was often tight, but God met every need. Looking back, we're glad for many of the things that we didn't have because it made us closer, it made us stronger and it made us lean on Jesus even more. We experienced joy, a lot of laughter and immeasurable love.

Danielle graduated from college and left home. One day we were talking when she said, "There's something I've wanted to tell you." She started crying and said, "I had an abortion." I, too, began to cry. My heart was breaking for her; she was shattered and in so much pain.

It doesn't matter whether your child is four or 40, there's nothing worse than seeing your child in pain and knowing there's nothing you can do about it. I felt so bad for her, for what she was going through and that she held on to the secret for so long. I had always told her that there's nothing she could ever do that would change my love for her. I wasn't angry or disappointed in her.

I understood that her decision was made out of a myriad of fears. I understand fear all too well. In my life I've found that when we walk through difficult times together it makes us closer, our bond greater and with that, love increases. Danielle is a strong, courageous woman and I have a profound respect and admiration for her.

She is married to a wonderful man and has four beautiful children. My heart smiles when I think about the fact that she's living my dream. God broke the chain of divorce and abandonment.

I want to share some thoughts. Things that I learned by being a single mom. I wish I had known some of these things during those years.

- It's not your job to be a perfect mom; it's your job to teach your children to need Jesus.

- Tell your children that you love them every day (even if it's through gritted teeth).

- Pray for your children every day.

- Go to church; we need to be in community with

Danielle & her mom, Mary

Jesus followers. That's where we find love and support, where we grow in knowledge and wisdom and most importantly, where we strengthen our relationship with Jesus.

• Jesus is with you; you're not forgotten, or being ignored.

• Jesus looks upon you with love and mercy. He isn't judging you. He declared you worthy at the cross.

• Ask Him anything—He's not holding out on you.

• Jesus is faithful and His faithfulness doesn't hinge on ours. He's faithful because that's who He is and He can't be anything else.

At right is a picture of Danielle (center), Simon, Mabel, June, Pearl, Otto and Mary, (far right). Danielle shares: "God has given me a passion to help women like me. I now help facilitate Bible studies. When I can't be leading a group I spend time praying over the ladies and facilitators. Over Christmas break I took my four kids to pick out items for Life Centers. It's important to teach my children about loving and caring for others and especially about Gods amazing Grace."

SOAR:
A Life-Changing Experience

CHAPTER 9 • Marilyn & John

Her Story

The Friday before Memorial Day in 1990, I ended my child's life.

I was a few weeks pregnant and my husband and I decided together that having a child at this time was impossible. Together, we drove to the clinic, which was in a poorer neighborhood across town. The clinic was a dingy gray-brown. There were no questions, just a crisp, clinical, impersonal efficiency from the admitting nurse. This made it easier to proceed. I was prepared for the procedure, stared at the ceiling and heard a buzzing, suctioning sound. Then it was over and I left with my husband. I remember feeling relief that it was over. With no more hard decisions we could get on with our busy, challenging lives.

Misinformed

It is hard for me to believe that someone who accepted Christ at a young age could come to believe that abortion was morally right. My parents grew up in the Depression; they cherished us but often talked about the financial burden of children. I realize that I formed a negative impression of having children. My teenage years were during the turbulent 1960's-'70's—a time of rebellion, violence, and rapidly changing values. A student leadership conference I attended at a state university indoctrinated me with ideas such as environmental responsibility by limiting family size. In college, many were sexually active and used birth control. If birth control failed, abortions could be obtained easily after Roe v. Wade passed; this seemed better than unwanted children. I married early and was employed at a state hospital caring for severely disabled people. I loved the people I cared for and their situations tore at my heart. *Would it be better if the most disabled had not been born?* These experiences and ideas led to my belief in the lies about abortion.

After a few years of marriage, I had two beautiful children who were my all. Times were hard, with financial deprivation and difficult living conditions. To change this, my husband went to school in an intensive program. We lived in a group home, where I was a houseparent. My husband was gone every day while I cared for the residents and my children alone. We faced severe marital challenges, but our growing faith in God, love and commitment helped us keep our family together. We relocated to another state and I completed a demanding professional program. We moved to a larger city, got jobs and bought an older home in a good school district. The children were happy.

We were in debt, but our prospects were bright. After a year, I landed my dream job. Then I became pregnant.

I did not want additional children. I was almost 40, had health risks, my job was demanding and there was no one to care for an infant. My husband was noncommittal; it was my decision. I felt I had done everything on my own with my first two children; I didn't see how I could do it now. I believed in the right to choose; that every child should be wanted. And I believed in protecting the environment. I would be ending the pregnancy very early. Conveniently, I believed that the child would not have a soul until it could survive on its own. So, I would be adhering to my Christian beliefs. The decision was made. Somewhere, a voice whispered, "You'll regret this," but I would think about that later.

The physical symptoms of the abortion passed after a long weekend. However, the empty feeling inside lasted. As our children grew, we became more involved in church. We wanted a family environment that fostered personal relationships with Jesus. As I walked closer to Christ, I heard sermons addressing the sin of abortion and I felt angry. Christians who believed abortion was a sin were misinformed, at best, but sometimes I would think about my loss. After my children left home, we became involved in leading a Christian group that required me to take a fearless and searching moral inventory of myself. It became impossible to ignore the Holy Spirit's conviction of my sin, but what could I do? I was ashamed, afraid and filled with grief. God tried to give me a precious gift, but I had refused it. When I looked in the mirror, I saw the face of a person who had shed innocent blood.

Again and again, I repented of my sin. I was (and am) so desperately sorry, but there is no going back. Through Bible study, praying and listening to the Holy Spirit, I came to believe that God had forgiven me, but I could not forgive myself. I knew God wanted me to accept His forgiveness, and that by not accepting it, I was putting myself above God. I needed help.

In the fall of 2017, my husband and I were at a very dark place in our marriage. As I asked God for help, I thought of my abortion. Perhaps God could use my sin to help someone else and that would help me. I looked for volunteer opportunities at Life Centers and I noticed SOAR, an abortion recovery program. It was an answer to prayer. It was hard to make the phone call; I had never discussed the abortion with anyone except my husband. I left a message and received a call back from a kind, empathic person with hopeful news. The next group that SOAR would undertake was for couples who had experienced abortion. When asked, my husband immediately said yes to SOAR. Could it be anything but God?

We had many marital issues, but the one God had us tackle together first was the issue we had been denying: the effects of the secret sin of abortion. Together, we sat at our kitchen table looking up scriptures and completing study materials. We didn't trivialize our sin nor take it lightly; the scriptures brought the full weight of our sin to our minds and hearts and we allowed the Word to work in us. We mourned and repented, together.

Together, we experienced God's kindness, patience, unfailing love and unconditional forgiveness. Together, we participated in group discussions with other couples who had chosen abortion. We were not alone in our sin, grief and regret. With others, we were able to experience healing and forgiveness. We were able to talk honestly about what we had done, admit our sin, express our repentance and experience healing. Because of SOAR, we were able to do what we had never felt worthy of doing: we mourned the loss of our child.

Together, we named our child. At the remembrance service, we memorialized our child, introduced him by name and shared our loss with others.

God kindly led us to **SOAR** to experience healing from our great sin. He used this as a beginning to heal other areas of our relationship. We will always regret not having our child. We mourn not knowing him or the grandchildren we might have had in this life. We do know he is safe in the arms of Jesus. We know that we are forgiven.

His Story

When I was in my late teens and early 20's, abortion was rarely a topic of conversation, at least among my family and friends. When the topic did come up, it would usually be related to stories of illicit abortions gone wrong. It basically was in the category of things "not done".

My first personal experience with abortion came in June, 1970. I had then been married to my first wife for four years and I had been on active duty in the military for 10 months. She informed me that she was pregnant, that she was not even sure who the father was and that she was making arrangements to get an abortion. With "help" and coaching from influential friends and acquaintances of hers, she was set to appear before several psychiatric evaluation boards to justify her decision. Although she did not share the details with me, evidently she was successful, feigning a complete mental breakdown if she could not end the pregnancy. Her decision to abort was approved. The event was scheduled at approximately five months. As it happened, I was home on emergency medical leave related to my father having major lung surgery. I drove her to Indianapolis for the procedure, which took many hours. (The procedure was a saline injection leading to labor resulting in expulsion of dead fetus). I waited in the parking lot as I could not be present. There was no sharing of feelings afterwards. My major feeling at the time was being even more distanced from her.

My first wife had her second abortion in November of 1970 in Washington, DC, where abortions were legal at that time. I was stationed nearby and we stayed together at the Fort for a couple of days. There was no talk of pros or cons that I can recollect. I was in my own head at the time and had no objections although it was "likely" the child was mine. I am sure that at the time I believed a child would have been an unbelievable complication to an untenable marriage, which ended two years later.

During the years following I did not think about abortion much or often. I did think that Roe v. Wade was a good idea—a reasonable solution to unwanted pregnancies, at least the way I understood it: that it was okay to abort in the first trimester, that it was up to each state to determine in the second trimester and that it was a no-go in the third trimester. Through personal experience, I came to believe that those who were outspoken against abortion were extremely self-righteous. I concluded that the ability of a single working mother with school-aged children to safely end an unwanted pregnancy was a good idea. I felt very self-justified in my thinking.

That was my basic belief when my current wife found out she was pregnant. A very big concern for me was her health. She had developed preeclampsia with our second child and was extremely likely to develop eclampsia if she carried this child.

In truth, I also felt a large amount of fear and frustration related to where we were at the time. My wife was just starting a professional career at around 16 years into our marriage, after much work and sacrifice on both our parts. I was in graduate school and working nights. Both of our children were in school. I believe we were in unison in thinking that another baby would be, at that point in time, a major complication. We both felt that ending the pregnancy was the best thing to do. I think I was numb and detached, having been hardened by my past history.

The day of the procedure I felt "cheap".

I rarely thought about the event during the years following. About 10 or so years later, after I had gotten much closer to God and Jesus (I had always been a Believer), I came to believe that God could and would forgive me/us, but that the loss of a child, a missing child, was and would be my punishment. I still have that belief: *I miss that child.*

When my wife first told me of the SOAR program I thought it would be a great idea. Going through the program far exceeded my expectations! The deep scripture study led me to a much better understanding of God's nature and of His forgiveness. Sharing with other couples and bringing the matter into the light put an end to the deep inner shame that I had felt. As the saying goes, we are, "only as sick as our secrets". All the elements of the program, such as acknowledgment, forgiveness, sharing and mourning, resulted in great healing. I recommend the SOAR program to all couples who have, on either or both sides, experienced abortion.

John and Marilyn are grateful followers of Jesus Christ. After careers in healthcare, they are both retired, spending time helping family members, including their daughters and grandchild. John enjoys carpentry and has recently finished the interior of their home with wood reclaimed from a 110-year-old farmhouse. Marilyn enjoys sewing and  *reading. They garden in summer and hike year-round. They are active in their local church and various ministries. Their mission is sharing how they have experienced God's power in healing the effects of their hurts, hang-ups and habits.*

Defined

CHAPTER 11 • *Deanna & Randy*

Her Story

Growing up, I attended a Methodist church in my hometown with my immediate family (parents and siblings) and extended family (grandparents, aunt and uncle and some cousins). I believed that being a Christian meant faithfully attending church on Sunday mornings and striving to be good.

As a young teen I attended a youth lock-in event where the youth leaders were vulnerable and shared about their own past sin. This was very helpful to me as my own family didn't offer such vulnerability.

I went forward to pray during this lock-in, believing that God was calling me to follow Him. I don't remember what I prayed, but I felt God drawing me to Himself.

There was no follow-up or discipleship happening in that church at that time and unfortunately, I did not make that youth group a priority in my life. I busied myself with academics, various clubs, band, and swing choir in my high school years.

I met my future husband, Randy, at 15-years-old and we began dating the following year. There were periods of time where we dated one another exclusively and other times where we "dated around". Upon entering a Christian college, I accepted a promise ring from him indicating that I would one day marry him.

During my freshman year in college, I again felt God drawing me to Himself through new friendships I was making, friends who loved Jesus. I wanted what I saw in them—an intimate, growing relationship with the Creator of the universe. I was curious how this was happening for them. Where was this dedication, passion and excitement coming from?

I saw differences in the Christian college compared to my public school experience. The professors opened their class time in prayer. My science professor spoke of creation vs. evolution. I was confused at this. I had a mixed batch of information between the secular teaching in my public school and a splattering of Bible stories in Sunday school. At college, Chapel was required for students, forcing time with God to be more of a priority. I thrived in this environment and recommitted my life to God, desiring a deeper relationship with Him.

Randy was back home working on his family farm. He too was growing in his faith through time spent with his brother. They had many conversations while farming together which soon turned into a type of discipling relationship.

We became engaged during my freshman year in college and got married in December of my sophomore year in 1984. In our search for a church home, we went to a small church, Trinity Wesleyan, for a period of time. We then joined a small body of believers within a "home church" environment. We spent time around a table on Sunday mornings studying God's word, singing worship songs and breaking bread together. It was a sweet time of growth in the Lord. I remember feeling that the scriptures were opening up, making more sense to me than ever.

Later we moved away from our hometown, down the road a bit, attending a Baptist church where we have remained for 30 years. We raised our family in this church and it has been instrumental in our growth in Christ.

Sitting in church one Sunday morning in February 2018, I found myself listening to a special speaker sharing on the topic of the sanctity of life. I was tracking with him very closely. He said a statement that was

profound to me. He said "When we don't talk about it, either abortion is not that bad or the gospel is not that good." I had never thought of it this way before. I believed this statement to be true, but knew my life was not demonstrating this truth. He was gentle and compassionate toward those who had made the choice to have an abortion. He invited anyone talk to him after the service. I felt he was giving me permission to begin talking about my past. I had prayed on several occasions and more in recent years for God to show me what to do with this pain, if anything *could* be done. I knew God was opening a door for me. I just needed to be obedient and walk through it.

You see, thirty-eight years ago when I was 18 years old, I had an abortion. This was a year to the month before Randy and I got married. Our first child together.

Reliving the Past

At the time of the pregnancy, I confided in one person—an older woman in my life. I went to her house late in the evening. She was awake, reading in bed. I fell on her bed in despair seeking her advice. She offered to tell my parents and to help plan a sweet, simple wedding. My response to her was that I could not do that. She asked, "Will you go to the doctor and verify your pregnancy?" I agreed.

I picked her up a few days after that, received confirmation that I was pregnant and asked for the information that I needed to have an abortion. I dropped her off after the appointment. I will never forget her words that afternoon: "Remember, you will need to live with this decision for the rest of your life."

Two weeks after learning I was pregnant, I was no longer. My initial reaction was relief. I went back to college after Christmas break. I took an ethics class where I had to study and write a paper on my viewpoint of three major topics—war, euthanasia and abortion. I took a stand against abortion while having had one a few short months earlier.

I moved forward with life not giving it much thought as I remember it. Life was busy with nursing school, work and marriage. Five years into our marriage, I remember feeling the weight of that decision when I became a mother for the first time. Holding and gazing into my firstborn's eyes, I knew there was one before her that I would never know or hold in my arms. It was my first remembrance of grief over this child.

Many years forward, I was the mother of five young children. My college friend, the one who greatly impacted me by her love for Jesus, came to visit. While sitting together in the car outside Walmart, we were observing two men holding hands as they entered the store. I remember either thinking or verbally expressing judgment toward them for their lifestyle choice. In that moment, God lovingly reminded me of what I had done and that I was no different than these men. We all are equally in need of God's forgiveness for our sin problem. The weight of my sin was so great in that moment that I confessed it to my friend. I physically became sick immediately following this conversation and had to go home and go to bed. She and I did not speak of it again.

More time passed. I thought about it more as the kids were becoming adults. I wanted them to know, but was paralyzed with fear at the thought of talking about it. Who could I talk to? Nobody knew. I was confused as to what was best and how to handle it. I was silently hurting. I had sought and claimed Christ's forgiveness multiple times—the first being in the abortion clinic before the procedure. But I had never practiced James 5:16 (GNT) "...Confess your sins to one another and pray for one another, so that you will be healed." I clung to this promise as I desperately wanted healing, if it was possible. I didn't know if I could expect to ever get over something this bad. I didn't know what this process was going to look like, but I was willing to trust God and obey.

The Key to Unlocking Silence

In 2018 when we had the special speaker at the church, I wanted to talk with him. When church was over, I stood around and talked with several people and then I looked around the empty auditorium. He was there, talking with another woman who was visibly upset. I carefully scanned the room to see who else was there—who might see me talking with him. I approached them with great trepidation, asking if I could interrupt long enough to get his contact information. He stopped his conversation with the other woman and approached me, looking into my eyes with compassion. He asked my name. I knew at that moment he *knew*. I felt such guilt and shame. He simply gave me his business card and said to call him anytime.

I called him the next day. I felt safe. He didn't know me. He could offer advice and possibly help clear my confusion. This way, I had options. I could listen and accept his advice or decline and go no further with it.

When we talked on the phone, I was full of emotion. I had not let these words come out of my mouth for others to hear. He listened. Offering understanding he said, "I would have done the same thing if I had been in your position." He went on. "One out of three women have had an abortion," indicating that I wasn't alone. This was astonishing to me. I grieved to think so many women were hurting the way I was. I instantly thought, *I have to work through this so I can help other hurting ladies.* Th most important thing he told me that day was, "I believe you can be healed," which gave me hope. I will be forever grateful for this.

I learned so much about unhealed hurts and forgiveness from the book, *Her Choice to Heal: Finding Spiritual and Emotional Peace After Abortion,* by Sydna Masse. In it, Sydna explains that the key to breaking out of our silent prison often lies in hearing someone else speak directly about abortion.

This is exactly what happened to me. I wanted out of this silent prison. I longed for spiritual, emotional and physical release. I hated the word abortion and never wanted to connect myself with the term post-abortive. The key that unlocked my silent prison door was hearing this man speak the truth to me with great compassion, encouraging me to talk to him. I was excited at the possibility of release, yet very fearful of the journey. I knew that in order for God to receive His glory in this messy story, I was going to have to start talking and seeking help.

The man of God connected me with a woman in South Carolina who authored a book on her abortion story. She talked with me the next day, sent me her book and connected me with my local Life Center, which offered post-abortive Bible study groups. A Bible study. *What a great way to do this?* I thought to myself.

In talking with the director of the SOAR program (Spiritually Oriented Abortion Recovery) from Life Centers, I had now confessed my abortion to three different people—all in one week—the week following that 2018 church service. Looking back, I am in awe of how God was caring for me, making quick provision through His faithful servants to meet me where I was and offer me encouragement, hope and direction. All I had to do was follow His lead and trust Him. The director of SOAR was expecting my call. My family was headed to to Florida for a two week vacation so we set a time to meet in three weeks.

In the meantime, I received the book, *Shattered into Beautiful*, in the mail as promised by the author. I couldn't wait to start reading it. I'd never heard another woman share her abortion story. I read it slowly, rereading parts of it, praying, crying and reading more. I was so grateful for her vulnerability; sharing her journey to healing and giving her counsel for others. I was like a child in a candy store with this book in my hands. I clung to every word. Through the pages of this book, I was able to spend time with someone who understood my pain. Not ready to talk to others about it yet, I only read the book when I was alone.

While visiting a family member on our way to Florida, we attended church in North Carolina. A song I had never heard before was sung during the worship time entitled, *I Am Defined[1]*:

> *I am not defined by who I was,*
> *I am defined by Whose I am,*
> *I am not defined by what I've done,*
> *I am defined by the blood of the Lamb.*

The words ministered to my soul as there was a great deal of guilt and shame that I was carrying. I needed God to remind me that I was not defined by this abortion, but by the blood of the Lamb. The gospel is so good! Out of His deep love for me, He offered His body as the perfect sacrifice for my sin in order to reconcile me to His Father and present me to the Father having no spot or wrinkle. I needed to keep this truth in the forefront of my mind as I walked this journey. I listened to that song frequently and thanked God for His very near presence and peace.

"...Christ loved the church and gave himself up for her, that he might sanctify her, having cleansed her by the washing of water with the word so that he might present the church to himself in splendor without spot or wrinkle or any such thing, that she might be holy and without blemish."
—Ephesians 5: 25-27 (ESV)

When I got home from vacation, I knew my next step was to confess this sin to others as the Lord led me. I started telling close friends, asking for prayer for the journey. Everything in me did not want to talk about this. I had this prevailing thought, *You did what you did so you would not have to talk about it.* In thinking about my motives, I think this was true. If I could have talked about it at the time, maybe I would have chosen a different option. Fear, guilt, shame and pride trapped me within this now silent prison. Ironically, 38 years later, the same issues I avoided then were still present. I needed to work through those issues in addition to working through the grief over my child.

I had to remind myself that God was clearly directing my path and I was going to trust Him. I could barely form the words with my mouth, I was so ashamed. I questioned whether I was doing the right thing each time I shared. Initially, I felt like I needed confirmation from those I told. I needed to know that they were okay and that our relationship would not change as a result of this new information. Constantly sick at my stomach during this time, my heart would start racing when I even thought about it. Each time I opened up to another person, I went home emotionally drained. Tossing and turning at night, I replayed the conversation in my mind. It felt like spiritual warfare. Satan did not want me to be free of this.

Then I began sharing with my kids. This took place over a couple of weeks. As each of my adult children listened and began processing the truth, they helped me process truth. The healing continued…

My oldest said, "So I'm not your oldest child?"

I paused, thought for a moment, and then said, "No, you are not."

My second oldest said, "So you have six children?"

Again I paused and then said, "Yes, I have six children."

These were truths I had never allowed myself to think. God gave me a greater understanding of His abundant grace through this journey. One of those moments was in the response of my fourth child. After bearing my heart and my heavy story, she paused and said, "Well, I think more highly of you now than I did before you told me…" She was giving me what I did not deserve—grace.

My youngest was silent. I asked, "Honey, are you okay?"

She said, "Mommy, why have you never told me this before?"

My response was, "I told you as soon as I could speak of it." I think she understood.

Last, but not least by any means, I planned to share my story with my son and his wife. I didn't know how this was going to work as they had two young children who would be present. My oldest daughter, who lived with us at the time said, "Mom, how are you going to do this?"

"I don't know," I answered.

"I will go with you and take the kids to the basement," she offered. My heart swelled with gratitude towards my daughter for her understanding and support. I sensed my God's very near presence providing the way. My son thanked me for sharing. I was finished...they all knew. I fell asleep on my son's couch holding his baby girl on my chest.

Each of my children extended grace to me. The following Sunday was Easter. Unexpectedly, all of my children were present with their spouses and children sitting around me in the church pews. In my own experience, any time a mother of adult children has all her children around her, it is an emotional moment; but this time had greater significance for me because they all *knew* and were still standing by my side.

When we were standing together I realized that I had feared their rejection, just as the books said. I don't think we have all been together in corporate worship at church since that day. It was not planned, at least not on my part, yet even more steps toward healing took place in those special moments together. I have a family picture of that Easter Sunday to remind me that God was very near, not only helping me, but going beyond what I could imagine or hope for. I was beginning to see His love for me was much deeper than I could conceive.

"For this reason I bow my knees before the Father...that according to the riches of His glory He may grant you to be strengthened with power through His Spirit in your inner being, so that Christ may dwell in your hearts through faith-that you, being rooted and grounded in love, may have strength

to comprehend with all the saints what is the breadth and length and height and depth, and to know the love of Christ that surpasses knowledge, that you may be filled with all the fullness of God." —Ephesians 3: 14-19 (ESV)

Three weeks had passed and it was time to meet with the director of the Life Center's SOAR program. She started by sharing her own abortion story, knowing that would be helpful to me. Then she asked for mine. I felt the floodgates open as I was finally able to express my pain and regret to someone who would understand.

Another statistic was shared with me that day. Eighty percent of couples who have an abortion together, do not stay together. She looked intently at me and said, "You are in the 20%."

Looking back now, my feelings were raw and unprocessed like it all happened yesterday. I had rarely let myself think about it, let alone talk to another person about it. It was like putting something in a box on a high shelf in the closet—you know it's there, but seldom, if at all, does one reach for it. Talking to her was like applying healing balm on a deep wound. I signed up for the next SOAR Bible study which started in a month. They offered us a couples class and my husband agreed to go through the study as well.

Realizing Grief

Again while reading *Her Choice to Heal,* I continued to have breakthroughs as I read the author's journey through abortion. Aside from reading her personal story of pain and loss, I began to see that the book was walking me through the stages of grief. Initially, I was surprised by this. I had not allowed myself to think about my loss or that I even had loss. I didn't often connect my abortion to a person—to my child. After 35 years, I was still stuck in phase one of grief: shock and denial.

The book spoke of this "wall of denial" and how we build it a few bricks at a time to protect ourselves, to cope with the reality of our decision (p.58, *Her Choice to Heal*). One of the bricks in my wall was dehumanizing my child. I remember thinking to myself before the abortion: *There is potential for life here, but as it is now, it could not live outside the womb. I can't relate to it as a human being at this point.* Even as a mother with five living children, I was still not able to acknowledge this life in a healthy way. Guilt formed another brick. I broke God's law, His plan for my sexuality and purity. Then I shed innocent blood to cover those broken laws. Other bricks were a compilation of fear, shame and self-focus.

As I read and walked through the stages, I remembered that time of my life. I felt desperate. The alternatives to abortion seemed too awful to contemplate. My rationalizing thoughts included: *What will this do to my family? I will disappoint my dad. I can't get married right now. I'm not ready to be a mother. How would my family treat Randy?* Sadly, I feared man more than I feared God and I allowed Satan to whisper in my ear, "If people knew about this, they would lose all respect for you and would not want to associate with you."

Fear and shame are crippling. They are tools that Satan uses to drive us away from God, but the truth is, when we seek the Lord, confess our sins and ask for His forgiveness, He releases us from fear and shame.

"I sought the Lord, and he heard me, He delivered me from all my fears. They looked to Him and were radiant And their faces were not ashamed."
—Psalm 34:4-5 (ESV)

And we do not have to live with guilt either.

"If we confess our sin, He is faithful and just to forgive us our sin and cleanse us from all unrighteousness."—1 John 1:9 (ESV)

Talking about it, forming the words with my mouth for others to hear helped me begin tearing down the wall of denial. I specifically remember walking away from a particular conversation not feeling the weight of the guilt and shame; they were melting away. Replacing them were hope and excitement about how God would use this in the future for His glory.

Songs with the theme of freedom in Christ ministered to me. Songs like, *Amazing Grace (My Chains Are Gone)* and others. My youngest daughter loves to sing. One day, she was bellowing out these words while working in the kitchen:

"I sing because I'm happy, I sing because I'm free.
His eye is on the sparrow and I know He watches me."[2]

I stopped in my tracks. "Grace, sing it again!" I said. I realized I was feeling happy because I was free. I was no longer carrying this burden.

"If the Son sets you free, you will be free indeed!" —John 8:36 (ESV)

Moving Forward

There was one area of denial I still needed to address—my child. It was time to let my child into my heart. Without consciously thinking about it, these were thoughts I had never allowed myself to entertain.

Was our child a girl or boy? Which one of our living children would he or she most have been like? What would this child be doing now? What would have been his or her struggles and strengths? What grandchildren are not here because of this decision? The questions could go on, each with an answer I would never know, at least this side of heaven. We were clearly the ones with great loss here.

As I began pondering these questions, allowing myself to grieve this loss, I felt very distant and removed from my child. The permanence of death was prevailing in my thoughts. In those moments God showed up again and helped me to think rightly about this situation. He reminded me that even though I destroyed my child's flesh, I could not destroy his or her spirit and that my child was alive and well in the arms of my Lord! He also reminded me that my life here on earth represented just a dot in time and eternity was a line. "You have eternity to spend with your child. Not a dot—a line."

Wow! My child is alive and well and has been all along! I have six children! Five on earth and one in heaven. In the big scheme of life, it will not be long before we can be together. A great deal of weight was lifted in these moments and more healing was taking place.

Our living children, helped me in this work of acknowledging and grieving the loss of our child. On Mother's Day, I received a very special gift—a birth stone necklace and earrings from our children. The note read:

> "This Mother's Day we wanted to honor the child whose loss you are currently mourning and whose presence each of us miss. Even though this time is hard, we hope it is also healing and hopeful. We love you, are proud of you, and are so glad that you are our Mom."

It was signed by all of our children and their spouses. They were showing me love so unconditionally. God's deep love for me was manifesting through our living children. This was God's grace and mercy on full display.

The birthstone was a Peridot—which is the stone for August—our child's birth month. My fourth child, Hannah, was not present when I received the Mother's Day gift. When I saw her later at a party, I leaned over and whispered in her ear, "Thank you."

Her response helped me move toward the acceptance phase of grief. She said, "Mom, I was so excited when I heard my sibling's birth month was August." I paused, confused a bit by her response. She continued, "I always wanted a sibling to share my birth month with. You know, Sarah and Grace share the month of June, and Bethany and Caleb share November. I never had a sibling to share my birth month with, and now I do!" I could hardly wrap my mind around what Hannah was saying. This detail about her sibling was significant to her and she was able to find joy in the moment.

"Thank you, Hannah, for this," I replied. "I want to get where you are. I want to rejoice in this life too!"

During the SOAR Bible study, I saw myself in a couple of stories from the Bible. The first was in 2 Samuel 11, where King David's sexual relationship with Bathsheba outside of marriage resulted in the shedding of innocent blood. Sending Bathsheba's husband, Uriah, to the front line of battle, knowing he would be killed, King David tried to cover his first sin. The second story was even more painful than the first. In

1 Kings 3:16-28, there were two women who brought one baby before King Solomon, both claiming to be the mother of the baby. They asked the king to decide which one would get the baby. King Solomon wisely said, "Cut the baby in half! That way each of you can have part of him," knowing that the real mother would never allow this to happen.

I was the woman who agreed to cut the baby in two; neither I nor anyone will have him. This was another moment of God displaying His amazing grace and deep love for me. He allowed me to understand, at a deeper level, the truth of who I am apart from Christ.

> *"The heart is deceitful above all things, and desperately wicked, who can understand it?"* —Jeremiah 17:9 (ESV)

Having never seen this before, I did not want to believe it about myself. In my pride, I thought too highly of myself. Better understanding the depth of my depravity has been a gift from God. In those initial moments of reflecting on this truth, I thought to myself —*this is hopeless! I have no defense! Where can I turn?*

Then my mind went to the Cross. Looking up from a prostate position, I saw my risen Savior who stood before me with outstretched, nail-pierced hands saying to me, "Now you are ready to receive my forgiveness."

The Lord of the universe has paid my sin debt. I am not getting what I deserve; instead, I am getting what I do not deserve. I have been given the opportunity to commune with the Great I Am, here on earth and forever, in heaven. I will be forever grateful for the sacrifice He paid, laying down His life on my behalf so that I could be judged as innocent instead of what I am—guilty.

Coming to terms with what I had done, tearing down the wall of denial and understanding there is nothing good in me, made it easy to receive the forgiveness He had been offering all along.

Unforgettable

Some of the highlights from the SOAR class my husband and I attended are unforgettable. We met with a class for six weeks, working through a Bible study entitled *Forgiven and Set Free*. The topics we covered were God's character, relief, denial, anger, forgiveness, depression and acceptance. There was a retreat at the end of the six weeks where everyone who had taken the class in various locations in the Indy area came together for three days. We had about 15 participants with equal amounts of facilitators who had gone through the study in the past. So everyone there had an abortion story. It was surreal. All ages, all walks of life, many different reasons for making this choice, all in different places as far as processing truth and healing.

During those three days, we watched a movie called *Tillie*. It's the story of a woman who had an abortion detailing her grief over loss in ways she couldn't understand. One of my takeaways from this story was this: these children know who their parents are and are waiting for their parents to acknowledge them. There are so many unacknowledged children. So many hurting mothers and fathers.

In a sense, that weekend we felt like we met our child and then let him or her go. We were asked to name our child, which acknowledges their personhood and then asked to publicly acknowledge our child as part of our family at a memorial service. These two steps were much hard than I anticipated—seeing my child's name in print and then forming the words for others to hear. Speaking truth to others is another step toward acknowledging truth to oneself.

We were issued a certificate of life that read:

Whereas, on or about the month of August 1984, a baby was expected to be born to:

Deanna Dawn Speer Overdorf, natural mother

Randall Kent Overdorf, natural father

Whereas, this child went to be with Jesus before birth. Be it known, the undersigned acknowledge the worth and dignity due this child:

Eternity Hope Overdorf

and who is acknowledged by the mother and father as a full member of their family and a creation equal with all other

human beings created in the image of God, having the same
inherent and immeasurable value.
This child lives eternally with Jesus and in the heart and mind of
the mother and father, now and forever.

I now have good news when I share this story. My loss is great. I am still deeply grieved over my sin, but God forgave even me before I asked. He loved me even as I was rejecting the life He created in me. He foreknew my need for a Savior and gave me Jesus. He has faithfully been by my side as I was hurting and suffering the consequences. He patiently waited until I was ready to work through all of this, orchestrating my readiness. He loved and welcomed my child into His presence. He has given me the gift of eternal life and the hope that I will see my child one day.

The last stanza of a poem taken from *A Gospel Primer*, talks about the great gift of salvation. This gift is my story, though I don't deserve it; but it is the gift that keeps on giving.

Remember that day in 2018? That Sunday, that special speaker's words that made such a great impact on me and helped me see more clearly the truth of the situation:

Abortion is really bad, but the gospel is so, so good!

His Story

If I ever get a girl pregnant, that is what I am going to do."

That was the line I heard that first introduced me to the word "abortion".

It was around 1971. I was nine-years-old and in the fourth grade. My friend made that statement in response to something the teacher had said, but that I didn't hear.

I had trouble grasping the concept or even what it meant and I had no idea the impact it would have just a few years later. I didn't know anything about sex. I remember thinking to myself, *what does he mean, if I ever get a girl pregnant?* But seeing the look on his face and hearing the tone in his voice, I remember thinking, *I need to remember this.*

About a year later I found some pornographic magazines of my dad's and some of my questions began to be answered—in the wrong ways and through all the wrong sources. So the downward spiral began at the young age of 10-years-old. My discovery lead to frequent sexual images invading my mind, premarital sex beginning at age 16 and three abortions by the time I was 22-years-old. Broken hearts, damaged and scarred emotions and a sin-infected pattern of thinking were casualties along the way.

I was not raised in a Christian home and we did not go to church. My parents were caring and moral people but mostly absent as I was growing up. From my earliest memories my mom suffered with severe depression and spent much of her life in bed. She rarely came out of the bedroom and when she did she would lie on the couch and sleep. For some reason I grew to blame myself for this. Our house was always very messy and quite often there was no food to eat because Mom couldn't go to the grocery to buy food. I remember feeling ashamed of our house and also ashamed of Mom, but I was also very protective of her, not wanting anyone to know about or look down on her or our situation.

My dad was a farmer who spent long hours working. He would come in late in the evening, very tired and not interested in spending time with me. I had two older sisters nearly 10 years older than me and they cared for me. They both married very young so by the time I was six or seven they were gone. I think this is when I first began having insecurity issues. I had very little structure or rules to follow. I remember wishing for more because I was a child who liked to please and rules gave me a way to do that. I remember thinking, *I wish they would just tell me what to do.* I craved affection, affirmation and assurance that I was doing what I was supposed to be doing. This craving fed my insecurities that developed into issues with anxiety and then later, depression and anger.

When I was about the age of 10, my dad decided to take my younger sister and me to a week-long revival meeting at a church down the road that some of my relatives attended. Every night I would sit and hear the preacher talk about the gospel, about how I was a sinner and needed forgiveness so I could go to heaven when I died. We would sing hymns of invitation at the end of the service. I went forward and prayed to receive Christ as my Savior. I was very sincere and I believed that I was saved and born again as a new creation in Christ, but after the week was over we never went back again.

So I did not grow spiritually or gain any knowledge of God or the Bible for many years. I believe that I was born again, but still very lost in my thinking and in my lifestyle. Life went back to as it was before and my insecurities and fears continued to grow.

By the time that I went into middle school, my anxiety and insecurity were beginning to dominate my life.

No Boundaries

When I stumbled upon my dad's pornography stash, it opened my mind to thoughts and feelings that I'd never had before and I did not know what to do with them. I felt an immediate pull and attraction, as well as curiosity and shame, but I would tell myself that if Dad was looking at it there must not be anything wrong with it. All of this set me up for years of struggle in the area of sexual temptation. Early on, viewing my dad's pornography led to a very active and unhealthy fantasy life. Then at age 16, soon after getting my drivers license, I became sexually active. Engaging in sex was, I thought, a way to satisfy these new desires, and seemed to help me in dealing with anxiety and insecurity. I think it helped to fill the void of love, physical touch and affection that I had craved for years and served as a temporary form of escape.

I began dating a girl who initially seemed to be just as interested in having sex as I was. She was very forward and aggressive about it and I had no resistance. It was not long before it became a habitual pattern of premarital sex. It was toward the end of my senior year that she told me she thought she might be pregnant. Together we went to see a doctor in another town who confirmed it. We were both filled with fear and didn't know what to do or where to turn. She was terrified at the thought of her parents finding out. I was also fearful of telling my parents.

Soon after I was talking with my younger sister. She could tell that I was not myself and asked me what was wrong. I broke down in tears and told her of my situation. She shared with me that she had been pregnant only one year before and that our mom had helped her get an abortion. She assured me that I should feel safe about going to our mom about it. At first I was not convinced, but after a few days my mom actually asked me what was bothering me. She was comforting and did not react in anger. She assured me that she would help me. Within days she drove my girlfriend and I to the abortion clinic and paid for it. Looking back I feel certain that my Mom was trying to help in a way that she thought was best, not knowing the damage it would cause or the regret that would follow.

Within a couple of years that same girlfriend and I became pregnant again. This time we got the abortion without involving any one else. I feel an even stronger sense of responsibility and deep regret because my girlfriend suggested we consider getting married and having our baby. But by then I felt strongly that our relationship had become very unhealthy and that we were not good for each other. In my mind our relationship was broken beyond repair. I told her I would pay for it and I drove her there. So we had our second abortion together.

It sickens me and rips my heart out to think about it now. It was a dark and selfish time in my life. I was not walking with God. My only consideration was what I wanted and what I thought was best.

Proverbs 14:12 (ESV) says, "There is a way that seems right to a man, but its end is the way to death."

By now God had graciously brought an amazing person into my life who would one day be my wife. Deanna was unlike anyone I had ever met. She was a true gift from God, one that He brought into my life at a time when I was probably at the lowest point in my life. I was heartbroken, living in sexual sin, full of anxiety, not walking with God. I could tell she was very different from any other girl I knew. I had an immediate respect for her that had been absent from my other relationship.

Yet my old habits and patterns were still with me. I pressured Deanna for a physical relationship. She normally resisted, but after a couple of years she became pregnant. She was very scared and didn't want her parents to know. She had plans that did not include having a baby at that point in her life. She was a freshman in college and had goals to graduate and become a nurse. Deep down I did not want to have another abortion but I was afraid to tell her about my past. Afraid that if I told her about my former girlfriend's pregnancies Deanna would no longer see me as someone she could one day marry. I knew I wanted to marry her and I was willing to do it right and keep our baby, but more than that I thought I should support her decision. So I willingly went along with her decision to abort our baby.

I felt a lot of guilt then; now I feel a lot of sorrow about it all.

I failed to protect Deanna and our unborn baby.

I am so thankful for the blood of Christ that washes our sins away. 1 John 1:9 (ESV) says: "If we confess our sins, he is faithful and just to forgive us our sins and to cleanse us from all unrighteousness."

God's grace and forgiveness enables me to face the reality of my wicked and sinful actions and choices. I am thankful for Psalm 103:11-12 (NLT) that says, " For as high as the heavens are above the earth, so great is his steadfast love toward those who fear him; as far as the east is from the west, so far does he remove our transgressions from us."

Moving Out of Denial

Even after the abortions, God in His mercy did not abandon me.

Deanna and I grew in our relationships with Christ and got involved in serving at church in many different ministries over the years. God blessed our marriage with five beautiful children. Life became very busy for many years.

I had confessed and received forgiveness for the abortions but after that, I buried those memories as deep as I possibly could, never wanting to talk about or even think about them. The thought of anyone ever finding out about them was terrifying to me. The only people that knew about them were my mom, my sister and a lady who Deanna had confided in. I hoped that nothing would ever be said and that no one would ever know. A couple times Deanna did ask me about the possibility of talking about it with someone and I would immediately respond with no. Never. Not ever. It was buried and I couldn't even think about it.

In truth now, I can see that I was living in denial. I didn't realize that deep down there were wounds in Deanna's heart as well as my own that would never receive healing unless we were willing to surrender it to God and be willing to bring the truth out into the light. God desired to bring healing but we first had to be willing to share what had happened with other people.

We had to acknowledge our sin and do what James 5:16 teaches: "Therefore, confess your sins to one another and pray for one another, that you may be healed."

In January 2017, God gave my wife the desire to go on a mission trip. We had just finished graduating our two youngest daughters from high school. God was preparing my wife for a new direction after having home-schooled our five children for over 27 years. He led her to a ministry of reaching out to sexually exploited women, in poverty and homelessness. At the same time God was working in her heart to get help for healing from our abortion of over 30 years earlier.

God led her to a ministry in June 2018 called SOAR (Spiritually Oriented Abortion Recovery). It is a part of Life Centers in Indianapolis. God used this ministry in our lives. For the first time we were able to openly acknowledge and talk about our abortion. We went through a Bible study with another couple and a facilitator. God taught me about humility, the need for transparency and the need to be willing to confess and talk about my sin. I needed to bring it into the light so that God could use it and bring healing. I was able to share things I had never even spoken aloud before. I experienced how coming out of denial and openly confessing sins truly opens the door for God's healing.

All of this began to bring healing into my relationship with Deanna. God has taught me humility and how to love sacrificially and put her needs above my own. This create oneness in our marriage.

God is a mighty Redeemer who can take our broken lives and stories, redeem them and use them for good! Our response is to be humble, surrender to Him and be willing to walk through the doors that He opens for us.

God uses our willingness to share our stories to bring healing to others as well as our own.

What a mighty God we serve!

Hello, my name is Deanna Overdorf. My life is full in this stage of life.

I continue working as an RN, now with Tendercare Home Health Care, one day a week caring for the health needs of pediatric patients in home settings.

I enjoy spending time with my grandkids weekly, whether in person or via FaceTime, reading books, doing crafts, singing songs, cuddling or helping with homeschooling.

I serve in a leadership role in a ministry called Alabaster Jar Indy. This ministry reaches out to women in the sex industry. We go into strip clubs, massage parlors, on the streets of Indianapolis and online, sharing the love of Jesus through gift giving and offering friendship to those who desire relationship.

I am wife to a faithful, loving husband and mother of five dear children and nine energetic grandchildren.

God has given me the desires of my heart and beyond. I am so grateful to my Lord and Savior Jesus Christ for patiently pursuing me with His deep love and drawing me to Himself.

I have been crucified with Christ. It is no longer I who live, but Christ who lives in me. And the life I now live in the flesh I live by faith the Son of God, who loved me and gave himself for me.
—Galatians 2:20 (ESV)

My name is Randy Overdorf. In December of 2020 I retired from the United States Postal Service after 31 years of service. Since retirement I have worked part-time as a transit bus driver for Riverview Hospital.

I enjoy camping ,kayaking, fishing, riding my motorcycle and watching sports.

I have served in many different ministries over the last 30 years including serving as a deacon for over 10 years at our church, as well as leading and teaching many different adult bible classes. My current passion in ministry involves serving on a leadership team of a Celebrate Recovery Group. I am also the leader of the worship team for CR.

In the last three years my wife and I have gotten involved with SOAR (Spiritually Oriented Abortion Recovery) which has been a wonderful blessing in our lives and has brought healing to our hearts and marriage. We hope God will use us in this ministry to help others in the same way.

I consider my most important role and ministry, in this season of my life, to be one of serving and supporting my amazing, gifted and beautiful wife in her passions and ministry calling.

We have been married for 37 years. We have five children and nine grandchildren for whom we are very grateful.

God has been merciful and so very good to us.

---

[1]Songwriters: Cox, Jihan & Chyka, Chloe. "I Am Defined." From the project: To: Gather. ©2015 Far Flung Tin Can
[2]Public Domain.

Fractured & Free

CHAPTER 12 • *Machelle*

I often wondered if my mom could hear me screaming. The pain was unbearable that day in that cold room of the abortion clinic in downtown Indianapolis. She sat in the lobby while I was in the next room having my baby stripped away from the very place he should have been safe. We were unaware of the depth of pain that our choice this day would have on us. Only time would tell the devastation of my decision, as well as the redemption of a merciful God; but not without first walking through some very difficult years.

This decision would not only affect me, but my mom, my dad and the rest of my family, including my family today. I really had no idea how it affected my mom until years later when she began to weep at a Sunday evening church service. She kept repeating, "Machelle, I'm sorry! I'm sorry." I asked her to what she was referring and she said, "The abortion." I am thankful that God eventually healed our hearts. Neither one of us understood that when we entered the abortion clinic our lives would be forever changed.

Walking into the clinic that day, I did not realize that I would never be the same again, unlike what they told us. Please know that doesn't mean that God is beating me over the head or punishing me. It just means that we cannot take a life without it affecting us for the rest of our lives in some way.

The abortion clinic told us both that I would be fine and that I would get on with my life. My mom and I fed into that lie. We were both scared. I was fifteen and my mom was thirty-eight. The fear was overwhelming. She had been a single mom for years and was now in a relationship with a man who was not good for her.

My pregnancy was not in anyone's plans and I did not, in fact, get on with my life. I dealt with my abortion in a very negative way through drinking, taking drugs and having more relationships. Depression set in and the shame of my decision was overwhelming to me. My thoughts toward myself were not good and I really didn't care if I woke up the next day. Again, I didn't fully understand the depth of what I had done, but somehow I did know what I had just allowed—someone to take a life from me on that cold January day of 1980. I would never be able to get that back. At least not on this earth.

Hurting In Silence

My heart hurt so badly, and I was not sure why. It would be years later before I would realize that a lot of my pain and behaviors were a result of my decision to have an abortion.

One story that I don't often share has to do with my little stuffed bear and my brother, Eddie Jr. The day of the abortion, Eddie Jr., who was always trying to protect me, went with us to the abortion clinic. He had no idea that I was inside having an abortion. He did not know that his baby sister's life was about to be changed forever. We told him that I had a doctor's appointment, so he stayed in the car and slept while my mom and I went inside.

After the abortion, I had a little stuffed bear and in my mind, that bear was my baby. My brother was, and still is, the one who is always teasing and playing jokes. One day, he took my bear and began to hit it. I remember going crazy: screaming, fighting, scratching and kicking him to get that bear out of his hands. Again, he did not know that I had an abortion or that I thought the stuffed bear was my baby. Suddenly, he stopped and looked at my mom and said, "Momma, what is wrong with Machelle?" She told him about the "doctor appointment". Eddie Jr. found out that I had allowed someone to take the life of his nephew by having an abortion.

After that, my abortion wasn't mentioned again until years later.

As time went on, the increased use of drugs, alcohol, and bad relationships continued, and the anger inside me was raging. There were many fights, car accidents and so many other unhealthy behaviors that surfaced as I didn't know how to deal with my abortion. I did not care about my life, whether I lived or died. It did not matter to me if I woke up the next day or not. However, every day I did thank God for waking me up and not allowing me to die in my sin.

After about a year and a half, I found myself pregnant again. So many thoughts ran through my mind. Here I was, now 16-years-old and pregnant again. I really didn't know what to do. I thought, *How is this going to work?* My mom was in a relationship with a man who she later married, who was abusive to her physically, emotionally and verbally. After she told him I was pregnant, he began to yell and scream at her. He told her that the bedroom I was staying in was not for me, it was for the baby that they would soon be having. I was listening to all of this from the other room. I cannot put into words how alone and abandoned I felt. All I knew was that the rejection and loneliness I felt that night from his words ran deep, and it would take a very long time to ever really heal. Wounds can lie dormant for many years.

I called my brother, who lived in Oklahoma where we were born, and asked him what he thought I should do. I had nowhere to go; nowhere to live. He was silent for a moment and then he said, "I don't know? Maybe you can go live with Gary and his family." (Gary was my baby's biological father). I called Gary and he talked to his mother, Violet, and her husband Johnny, and I moved in with them. We would later live with his sister, Teresa. I will forever be thankful to Violet, Johnny, and Teresa for allowing me to live with them and giving me a safe place to have my baby, Brandon.

Gary and I eventually got our own place. Our first apartment was a one-bedroom that had so many mice in it, I'm still terrified of mice, even to this day. One day after several traps were set, they all started going off one by one. It freaked me out, to say the least! But my heart was full of love with Brandon. He was the cutest, sweetest, most adorable little brown baby in the world. I loved and adored him then and I love and adore him now. (Now he is just a bigger version of that sweet, brown baby and I still think he is the most handsome young man I know.) Brandon was my world at that time. Through a lot of crazy circumstances, Gary and I did not make it. We both had a lot of issues and neither one of us knew the Lord. We went our separate ways and when that happened, as a young mom, I did not think it was a big deal. I realized years later that it was a big deal for Brandon. The mistakes and choices that we make affect many things. I would soon realize my need for the Lord in my life.

The Pressure Of Being A Single Mom

I was working double shifts trying to make it. I had no education and a little toddler who was depending on me. The place I worked allowed me to work two shifts selling coupon books. (Yes, be kind to the telemarketers—you have no idea why they are doing what they are doing on the other end of the phone.) One thing that I knew I could do well was to talk, so I sold coupon books and helped the office with payroll. It was a joke for me to do payroll, but I did it, and did it well for being so young with no training.

Now I know that all of my success in those tasks was the Lord giving me the ability to accomplish them. In that little office space on Michigan Street in Indianapolis, God began to place people in my path. Carolyn Nichols would be one. She would always invite me to church. There was a delivery guy who would always invite me and the entire office to church. After several attempts and invites, I went to church with Carolyn. I felt a little out of place there, so I didn't go back. Looking back, I know she prayed for me to at least go somewhere.

I decided to go with the guy in the office who was inviting EVERYONE to church all the time. Some of the people in the office had been going with him and said it was a nice place to go. I didn't want to go with him, as I didn't really trust men at this point in my life. However, I went and Brandon loved it.

After church Brandon came running to me from Children's Church with his little papers and a big smile on his face. I knew that because of Brandon I would go back, and we did. At the time it was called Southwest Church of God and the Pastor was Terry Harris.

I was truly scared walking in because I thought the walls were going to fall in. Looking back I can tell you that God was doing something in the midst of all of that. I had gone a few times when I saw a lady I knew named Linda, who I had worked with for a short time. I know God was in all of it. We make our plans, but He orders our steps.

I remember Linda gave me a big hug and that helped calm some of the fear and anxiety that I was feeling at the time. She still gives big hugs as she is still very much a part of my life. I would not realize until years later that she would end up being a lifetime friend and mentor, to my 32-year-old daughter, Briana. Linda and her husband Tom are instrumental to our family and have been there for all of us in every situation. They were and are truly sent from God.

A Day of Salvation

Every time I was at church, Pastor Harris would give an altar call after the message. He did this so that anyone who wanted to receive Jesus as their Lord and Savior could come down front and pray. Every Sunday Pastor Harris would give that altar call and the guy next to me, who had invited me to church, would ask me if I would like to go down and pray. I would always look at him and say, "NO." This went on from February of 1986 to August of 1986.

In August of 1986, another altar call was given and again the guy who invited me asked me if I wanted to go and pray. Again, I said, "No," but this time in my heart, I really wanted to receive Jesus. However, I did not say a word to him. I stood there not moving but wanting to move when a couple from across the church named Skip and Jackie came over to me. Skip said, "Young lady, the Lord told me you really want to give your life to Him." Although I didn't know a lot about the Lord, this I did know; the Lord had to have told Skip and Jackie this because I really wanted to go down front and surrender my life to Christ. I just didn't want to go with the guy who had invited me to church. I didn't want him to think I was doing anything for him. Remember, I did not trust men at this point in my life.

That morning in August of 1986, I prayed and asked Jesus into my life. One of the first things that I asked God, was to please forgive me for my abortion. Of course, all of this was under my breath where no one could hear me. I somehow knew that I was forgiven of my abortion and all those other things. However, looking back, I know I was not free. I would soon realize that there was much more to accepting Christ as my Lord and Savior than I thought. That was the start of my healing, but I had no idea at the time.

Life went on and I grew in the Lord. Two years later I married the guy who invited me to church. After we had been married a year he adopted Brandon. We had to be married that long for him to adopt Brandon. Then we had our daughter, Briana.

Battle For My Life

Again, life seemed to be going along well, or so I thought it. I did not realize at the time that my life was getting ready to change in a drastic way. Suddenly, I seemed to get very angry and depressed. I tried to put on a happy face but was unable to do that even in the secret, quiet place of my home. No matter how good things seemed to be going, I was still struggling with depression. I couldn't figure it out. I kept thinking, *I'm saved, so life should be good.* I should have been okay, but I wasn't. I didn't know it then, but I was getting ready to take on the battle of my life.

As the days, weeks, months and years went on, I continued the fight against depression. It seemed that I could not shake it. No matter how hard I prayed and worshiped the Lord, I could not shake the feeling. I felt like every time that I was trying to get out of depression, I would hit a wall or a ceiling. I now know the enemy of my soul was trying to destroy me. It got to a point where I didn't want to live.

I started remembering the abortion I had when I was fifteen. *Why now?* The enemy kept telling me that if Steve, my husband, found out that I had an abortion, he would divorce me because I entered the marriage with a lie. I had not told Steve about my abortion. Very few people knew about my abortion, and I didn't think I could ever tell Steve, or anyone else for that matter.

Steve and I came from what I called two different sides of the tracks. He grew up in church and had a two-parent family and I didn't. I was so afraid to tell him, as I had heard his mom say, "I think any woman who has had an abortion ought to have her tubes tied!" Oh, how that comment felt like I was being stabbed with a knife.

I'm thankful that God healed the relationship between his mom and me and she became one of best "cheerleaders" in my life. My mother-in-law had no idea that I had an abortion at age fifteen. I could not tell anyone at church, especially my husband. I felt too ashamed to do so. This is where the secrecy of abortion will bind you. The enemy loves to quiet us.

The Battle Continued

As time went on, my depression continued, even to the point of me writing a letter to Steve that I was unable to handle life. Really, it was the abortion aftermath, and I could no longer live with the guilt and shame. I was going to end my life. Repeatedly the enemy was in my ear telling me life after lie. He told me that my children would be embarrassed of me, and over and over again that Steve would divorce me. I was terrified to say the least. I am so thankful that the Lord intervened, and before I took the bottle of pills, Steve called and said he was thinking about me and that he loved me. I now know the Holy Spirit was working. Somehow, I knew it was a sign from God. I emptied the bottle of pills and tore the letter up.

This was going to be a journey. I was not sure what the next step would be, but I had made my mind up that I was going to live and not take my life! I proclaimed I will live and not die and held onto God's promises in the Bible. When I look back and think of what could have happened had I taken my own life, I weep and fall on my knees at the mercy of God and His goodness and grace.

No More Secrets

After that encounter with God in our home, we were at church the next Sunday in the evening service. Our pastor, Terry Harris, was preaching on oppression. I knew as I sat there listening to his message that I was being oppressed by the enemy. I wasn't that familiar with spiritual warfare, but I was getting ready to get schooled in it.

At the end of the message, Pastor Harris invited people to come up for prayer. He said anyone who is being oppressed by the enemy needs to come forward. I knew that the thoughts and plans for suicide were from the enemy, so I went forward. There was a prayer line. (Today, we call these prayer teams, and I am thankful to be a part of one in our church.) That night in the prayer line, there was a little prayer warrior and spiritual mother of the church whose name was Kate. I got in front of her. This little lady was maybe five-feet-tall. She looked at me and asked, "Honey, what is it?"

At that moment, I thought my heart would stop, as I had not spoken to anyone yet about my abortion, including my husband Steve. Only a few people knew. I was speechless. I just stared at her. She placed her hand on my heart and said, "Whatever it is, you have got to get out." All at once I blurted out, "I had an abortion! Before I had Brandon, I had an abortion!"

This prayer warrior looked at me and truly responded to me the way Jesus would. She said, "It is under the blood! Under the blood of Jesus!"

I said to her, "I know it is, but I'm still hurting and I don't know what to do." She said she was going to send me to Pastor Harris, who was praying for people as well. The way this little lady responded to me gave me enough courage to go to Pastor Harris.

As I look back and think about it all, she was probably thinking, "This lady needs the 'big dog'." I went and shared with Pastor Harris that I had an abortion before I had Brandon. I could have kept this all hidden. I had Brandon so young and no one would have ever thought that I would have been pregnant before that, at age fifteen; but God had different plans. He wanted me to not only be forgiven, but to be set free!

Pastor Harris began to pray for me, and then after praying for me he asked me a question that has forever changed my life. "Have you told Steve?"

"No, I haven't." He told me that I needed to tell him. I was still so afraid to tell Steve because the enemy kept feeding me lies about him divorcing me. I was scared that I would lose this man. A man that I truly had fallen in love with and did not want to lose. I didn't want to tell him for fear of losing him, but I also knew I could not live with this secret inside of me anymore. I needed to tell Steve and I was going to tell him that night before we left the church. I had to tell him and get it out. As I look back, I see that God had ordered it all.

I went to Steve while he was playing the drums and I told him. It was the hardest thing that I've ever had to tell him, but I knew it had to be done. After I told him I had an abortion before I had Brandon, he just hugged me and said we would get through it.

I thank God because Steve has my back in prayer. Every time I go somewhere and share, Steve prays for me. If he cannot be with me when I go to speak, he is praying for me. He's my biggest supporter outside of Jesus.

My life is still healing, and will always be healing this side of Heaven, as one of our ladies shared in a "Forgiven and Set Free" Bible study. But one thing I know for sure; I will never again be paralyzed by the secrecy of abortion.

Today, although my life is not without trials, I am able to live and walk in freedom regarding my abortion. This has helped me walk in freedom in other areas of my life. The Lord has allowed me many privileges and honors throughout the years; one of those is being Steve Montgomery's wife! He has been and is patient with me even still today. I know without a shadow of a doubt he will always love me. The other is being a mom to my two children, Brandon (Lauryn) Montgomery and Briana (Andrew) Howe, as well as being a Gramsie to the sweetest, most precious Grands in the world.

The other honor was being able to take care of my mom when she was terminally ill. My mom passed away at the young age of fifty-six. I had the privilege, although very difficult, to take care of her. I know she is now with my son, her grandson, in Heaven, having some in-depth conversations, I'm sure.

I also have been given the unique privilege to be on staff at Life Centers, formally Crisis Pregnancy Center, for 20 years. I am a Center Director at one of our six centers in Indiana and I coordinate our Post-Abortion Program, known as "SOAR" (Spiritually Oriented Abortion Recovery (formally called GRACE)). I lead those studies, the weekend retreats and have memorials for both men and women, as well as family members who have been touched by abortion.

Life is not perfect, nor does it come without difficulties. But oh, what joy it is to be in the place God has called me to be…His will! I know He has created me and all of us for His purpose and His glory. I pray that if you do not know Him today as your Lord and Savior, that you may be pointed in His direction from something that you read in this book. May you allow the One who can heal to heal, and as you are forgiven, remember to walk in that forgiveness, as well as the freedom Jesus has given. I am truly privileged to be a part of the plan that He has for His people. May my life, as well as yours, be a reminder to all that God wastes nothing!

Machelle Montgomery has served on staff with Life Centers (formally Crisis Pregnancy Center) of Indianapolis for 20 years. In this capacity, Machelle has served as Center Director, and has lead the "Abortion Recovery Program" for all six centers. She has also spoken internationally as a workshop leader for "Ramah International Conferences".

Machelle is well respected within the pregnancy center movement as a leader in abortion recovery efforts. She has been married to her husband for thirty-three years. They have two adult children and eight beautiful grandchildren, who are full of life, with number nine on the way!

Machelle speaks at women's conferences as well as churches across the nation. She is also involved with "Anchorsaway Ministry" and CEO, Nancy Fitzgerald. "Anchorsaway Ministry"is a college preparation Bible study that prepares students for the future. Their curriculum has been published in the nation of Turkey, along with DVDs of Machelle sharing her testimony.

Through "SOAR" (formally "GRACE") the abortion recovery program that Machelle coordinates, both a men's and couple's program have been established. The couples program ministers to those who aborted together before marriage or while married and are still together. Several couples have successfully completed this program with the evidence and testimony of God's freedom in their lives.

Even through these are accomplishments, the greatest honor for Machelle is being a wife to Steve Montgomery, a mother to her children, and the "Gramsie" to her

Grands!! Machelle says those are the true treasures which God has graced her with, and for that she will be forever grateful!

Hope Possible:

BE HEARD. BE SEEN. BE FREE

*W*ithin every chapter of this book, both men and women found help at just the right time.

Are you pregnant or do you think you may be?

A pregnancy can seem overwhelming. There are many pregnancy centers throughout the United States that offer pregnancy tests, support and will present you with options. You do have choices. Reach out to be informed and make the decision that is right for you.

Use the numbers and information below as a resource or Google "pregnancy centers near me" to find someone in your area. Reach out any time, night or day.

Nationwide Call or Text: 1-800-712-4357
Visit OptionLine.org to chat online.

Have you had an abortion and feel like there's no hope?

If you've read the pages of this book, our hope is that you see a light breaking through the darkness—a glimmer of hope. SOAR (Spiritually Oriented Abortion Recovery) is the program used by many of the people in this book, but it all begins with a conversation. Reach ut to Machelle using the information below, no matter where you are in the United States.

Call or Text: 317-714-0919
or email: mmontgomery@lifecenters.com

You don't have to wait.

You may be facing fear. You may have anxiety. You may think you've gone too far for God to ever love you, let alone see you; but you *are* seen.

He loves you—no matter how far away you feel.

You can pray now and Jesus will hear you. Prayer is like talking. It might feel like your talking to yourself, but when you call on Jesus, He hears you.

Even if all you can say right now is, "Jesus, I need you." Just start there.

You may be ready to begin a relationship with Jesus today.

In the Bible, Gods road map for life, John 3:16 (ESV) tells us, "For God so loved the world, that he gave his only Son, that whoever believes in him should not perish but have eternal life."

Believing in Jesus isn't about religion, rules or rituals. It's about a relationship. Jesus Christ wants to be your best friend; He wants to talk with you all the time. God made you for a relationship with him!

You won't be rejected. The Bible promise us in the book of Romans Chapter 10, verse13 (NIV): "Everyone who calls on the name of the Lord will be saved."

If you're ready to give your heart to Jesus, you can start by praying this prayer:

"Dear Jesus, you promised that if I believe in you, everything I've ever done wrong will be forgiven and you will accept me into your eternal home in heaven one day. Thank you that I can be sure you will fulfill your promise, that I can be assured of my salvation.

"I confess my sin, and I believe you are God, my Savior. I receive you into my life as my Lord. Today, I'm turning every part of my life over to you. I want to follow you and do what you tell me to do.

"Jesus, I am grateful for your love and sacrifice that makes it possible for me to join you in heaven. Thank you that I don't have to earn or work for my salvation, because I know that is impossible. Please accept me into your family. In Jesus' name I pray.

Amen."

If you prayed that prayer, you are a Christian! You have a relationship with Jesus. We're so happy for you! Please reach out and let us know how we can help you on your new path in life!

Call or Text: 317-714-0919
or email: mmontgomery@lifecenters.com

Prayer adapted from Pastor Rick Warren (pastorrick.com/settle-your-salvation-today/).

CPSIA information can be obtained
at www.ICGtesting.com
Printed in the USA
JSHW021032200322
23969JS00005B/4